D0387524

One-Minute Devotions for Dads

One-Minute Devotions for Dads

Jay Payleitner

EUGENE, OREGON

Cover by Left Coast Design, Portland, Oregon

ONE-MINUTE DEVOTIONS FOR DADS

Published by Harvest House Publishers
Eugene, Oregon 97402
www.harvesthousepublishers.com

ISBN 978-0-7369-4475-5 (padded hardcover)
ISBN 978-0-7369-4476-2 (e-book)

Printed in China

12 13 14 15 16 17 18 19 20 / RDS-SK / 10 9 8 7 6 5 4 3 2 1

To each of the thousands of dads I've met.
And those I will soon meet.
Keep being the awesome dad your kids deserve.

Acknowledgments

While I was working on this project for dads, my own dad passed away. He lived with grace, thoughtfulness, and humor. He died well. The bone and liver cancer must have been painful, but he never let on. I will cherish every memory of him, especially the spiritual conversations we had over the last few years. I look forward to spending even more time with him in heaven. His quiet strength and influence can be found throughout these pages. I miss you, Dad.

I'm honored also to list another group of fathering advocates that have greatly impacted my life as a dad and follower of Christ: Carey Casey, Brock Griffin, Steve Wilson, Bea Peters, Cathy Henton, Sherri Solis, Brian Blomberg, and Eric Snow of the National Center for Fathering. Plus Ken Canfield, the founder, and the late Peter Spokes, who served with distinction as president of the National Center for some 15 years. For more than two decades, I've been working alongside this team, co-writing and co-producing *Today's Father*, a daily three-minute radio program, and it's still going strong on hundreds of stations. Announcer Jerry Hutchinson and engineer Joe Mills have also worked on this broadcast since the beginning.

Other dads have contributed to this devotional, most notably Paul Gossard, editor extraordinaire. Thanks also to Bob Hawkins Jr., Terry Glaspey, and LaRae Weikert at Harvest House, who challenged me with this project.

Most importantly, I'm humbled to surrender any impact this manuscript may have to our heavenly Father. He promises to meet all our needs. Often in ways that we least expect.

~

This is not a typical devotional. Sorry to disappoint. I set out to be all serious and preachy, but I just couldn't do it. All the dads I know already have enough stuff in their life clawing for their attention. I didn't want to burden you with one more task on your must-do list.

So instead, I did what I do best. I took a serious project and had fun with it. The book is filled with truths critically needed by all dads everywhere. But the process of taking them in and putting them to work on behalf of your family will not be a painful proposition. I promise.

This book is a twofer. It's a devotional for you, Dad. But the chief beneficiary is going to be the kids you love so much.

Having spent more than 20 years researching and writing for fathers, I know that no two dads are alike. Some men are natural connectors. Some men are lone wolves. Some dads feel like they're looking in a mirror when they see their son. Some dads think, *Where did he come from?* Maybe your daughter is Daddy's little princess. Maybe she's a tomboy, a bookworm, or a free spirit.

In every case, my first wave of advice is the same. Be there. Enter their world. Invite them to enter yours.

That's the only way you'll know your son's or daughter's gifts, talents, and dreams. How they're wired. What makes them unique. That information is tremendously important as you come alongside them as the primary person God has assigned to help them reach for the stars.

How to describe these 140 devotionals? Each one stands on its own. There are thought-starters and idea-finishers. You'll dig through memories that look back and discover big-picture thinking that will help you look forward. Included are references to movies, TV shows, books, sports, current research, historical events, parables, heroes, and biblical passages you'll find familiar, and some not so much.

Every time I sat down at my keyboard, I asked God to help me give dads something they would actually use. Along the way, I smiled, grimaced, laughed out loud, brushed away a tear, and made some new personal discoveries.

If you let it happen, you just might be challenged, equipped, humbled, encouraged, inspired, and refreshed and gain a new sense of gratitude and awe when it comes to God's plan for fathers.

When you're done, you'll be a better dad. I know because I am a better dad for having written it.

I'd love to hear which of these devotions made a difference to you and yours. To track me down or to read my dadblog, go to jaypayleitner.com. Thanks.

LIFELONG HERO

"When I was a boy of 14, my father was so ignorant I could hardly stand to have the old man around. But when I got to be 21, I was astonished at how much the old man had learned in seven years."

MARK TWAIN

To a four-year-old, a dad should be a bit of a superhero. Young kids need to feel safe and secure. Dad needs to be the strongest, smartest, bravest guy in the world.

If that seems like a lot of pressure, don't worry, Dad. Sometime in the following six or eight years, that perspective is going to change. You will relinquish your mythological superhero status. And really, that's a good thing.

To raise well-adjusted teenagers, dads need to become human and even vulnerable. You're still an authority figure. You still know more than they do on most topics. Teens still depend on Dad for protection and provision. But the relationship shifts from fiction to fact. For fathers of teens, respect comes not from being invincible, but through your ability to lead, solve problems, persevere, overcome challenges, and even admit when you don't have all the answers.

That kind of relationship allows your growing children to respect you as a father, a real person, and a follower of Christ. As you and your children begin to establish an adult relationship, it also makes it easier for you to respect them. And teens need to feel respected.

Too many parents buy into the myth that raising teenagers is seven years of thankless toil and mutual contempt. Don't believe that lie.

Done well, the teenage years are just the beginning of a give-and-take relationship between fathers and their growing children. It can bring tremendous satisfaction. Having a sustained one-on-one connection with your adult child is even greater than opening a report card with straight A's or watching your son or daughter hit a walk-off home run. Really. I'm not kidding.

What about you?

Parenting doesn't end when kids leave the nest. If you've laid the foundation properly, fathering just gets better and better. It's more joy for less work.

A LITTLE AT A TIME

"These commandments that I give you today are to be on your hearts. Impress them on your children. Talk about them when you sit at home and when you walk along the road, when you lie down and when you get up."

DEUTERONOMY 6:6-7

Over the years you have picked up a handful of truths, some core values, and a few strategies for surviving this world and thriving in the next. Some you were taught. Most you learned the hard way. All of which you want to pass on to your children.

How does a dad convey these lessons without lecturing or facing a barrage of blank stares or eye rolls? The secret is to deliver those truths a little at a time as life unfolds. Don't wait for just the right moment or the perfectly planned weekend to transfer all your bits of collected knowledge in a single grandiose and laborious speech. Instead, gently and consistently "impress them on your children." Notice that the command isn't to bash them over the head or shriek into their skulls. It doesn't say nag, cajole, or fume. The word "impress" suggests images of lovingly leaving a permanent, noteworthy imprint or trace. Having made your mark in their life. Almost like an artist signing a fine oil painting.

How? It's spelled out nicely in the verse. Talk to them during the regular course of life. At the kitchen table. During commercial breaks. Strolling down a dirt road. Tucking them in at night. Chatting over waffles.

Make it an ongoing conversation. Leave 'em wanting more. If a question comes up you can't answer, that's okay. They know you'll weave in and out of their days with fresh insight, thought-provoking follow-up, and a listening ear.

What about you?

God wants to talk to you the same way, Dad. Sitting at home. Walking along the road. When you lie down. When you get up. Are you listening?

DUMPING ALLOWED

"To listen well is as powerful a means of communication and influence as to talk well."

JOHN MARSHALL (1755–1835)

Want to communicate to your kids that you care? Listen.

If you think you're pretty good at listening then you shouldn't be afraid of this little test. Ask yourself, *When's the last time my child came to me with a question or problem?*

If you're not a very good listener, your children may have learned long ago not to bother you because you don't really listen anyway—all you do is lecture and then go back to what you were doing before you were interrupted.

Maybe that suits you just fine. You don't want to be a dumping ground for their problems. But be warned. If your kids need to talk about something they are going to find someone to talk to. They will find someone who will listen. And that person will offer advice. And it could be bad advice leading to tragic results.

It may be that listening doesn't come naturally to men. It feels like a passive activity, and we're action-oriented. The solution? Practice active listening. Ask questions. Nod. Make eye contact. Get clarification.

Rephrase their words back to them, so they know you really hear what they're saying. Don't be too quick with answers. Make it a point to pause before giving advice.

The art of listening may be one of those secret parenting skills that moms have over dads. With a little practice, you can do even better than her.

Speaking of your children's mom. Listening is a good way to communicate that you care about your wife as well. But you already knew that.

What about you?

Maybe you're the kind of guy who likes to lecture. That can be an effective parenting style, especially if you lecture from an informed perspective. And how do you get informed? You listen. In other words, listen first, and your lectures will have much more impact.

LET 'EM FLY

"Children are a gift from the Lord;
they are a reward from him.
Children born to a young man
are like arrows in a warrior's hand.
How joyful is the man whose quiver is full of them!"

Psalm 127:3-5 NLT

This is an image on which you could meditate for hours.

You're an archer. You are young, strong, and confident. You reach over your shoulder and extract a single arrow from your quiver. You crafted that arrow with care and packed the quiver yourself, so you know the shaft is straight and true, the feathered fletching precise. Still, you slide your fingers down the narrow cylinder in preparation for a flawless fight. You've spent many hours disciplining yourself, and so it feels natural to slide the notch of the arrow onto the bowstring. Combining strength and gentleness you pull that arrow toward you. Close to your heart. With great care you choose a target that's exactly right for this exact arrow. You remain steadfast, feet planted firm. With a slight smile you let the beloved arrow fly, your assignment as a warrior complete.

That was so much fun. You do it again. And again.

With each one of your kids. Until your quiver is empty. Just as God planned.

What about you?

Open your Bible and read all of Psalm 127. It's a stunning opus dedicated to all you do and all you are as a father. Here's an idea: It's only about a hundred words. Memorize it and you can meditate on it anytime you like!

PRACTICE MAKES PERFECT

"God is not saving the world, it is done. Our business is to get men and women to realize it."

Oswald Chambers

When's the last time you led someone to Christ? If a conversation with an unsaved friend turns to spiritual matters, do you have a script in your head explaining the simple yet profound doctrine of grace? As believers, the ability to speak coherently about Jesus is in our job description. "We are...Christ's ambassadors, as though God were making his appeal through us" (2 Corinthians 5:20).

The facts are readily available. Everybody sins. Sin separates us from God. Somebody has to pay for our sins. God loved us so much that he sent his Son to pay for our sins. It's a free gift. All we have to do is believe and accept it. There's not much more to it than that.

With a little effort you could find some supporting Scripture and be ready to deliver the plan of salvation to anyone at any time and anyplace. All you need is someone to practice on. Do you know someone who looks up to you and will listen to you while you get the words right? Maybe someone who needs to know about grace themselves?

Dad, your kids need Jesus too. And it's a rush—and a privilege—to be the one who helps them take that step of faith into God's kingdom.

What about you?

If you didn't know, this is the most important devotion in this book. For you. And for your kids. And for your neighbors. And for your enemies.

THE SMARTEST MAN IN THE WORLD

"Those who are older should speak, for wisdom comes with age."

JOB 32:7 NLT

I was nine years old. It was the annual Payleitner pilgrimage to the shrine at the corner of Clark and Addison Streets. When I was growing up, my dad made sure we made it to at least one Chicago Cubs doubleheader every summer. One of the great traditions for my brother and me was filling out our own scorecards with two fresh, sharp Cubs pencils purchased from one of the vendors just inside the Wrigley Field turnstiles. In the 1960s, the scorecards were a quarter and the pencils were a dime. We never asked our dad for foam fingers, Cubs pennants, or Billy Williams jerseys. We knew that the scorecard and pencil was our souvenir. And that was enough.

About the second inning, tragedy struck. My pencil lead broke. Of course I could sharpen it at home, but how was I going to complete my traditional duties tracking Kessinger, Beckert, Williams, Banks, Santo, Hundley and company? I couldn't ask for another pencil, could I?

I showed the unusable writing utensil to my dad and he didn't miss a beat. He took it and within 20 seconds handed it back sharpened and ready for the next batter. You may be able to guess what he did. To an adult, it may seem obvious. But to this nine-year-old, scraping that pencil at just the right angle with just the right pressure against the concrete floor of the grandstand was nothing short of brilliant. My dad was a genius!

Dad, take advantage of those years when you know more about life than your kids. Solve the occasional minor crisis. Display wisdom. Be a humble hero. Store up your genius points so you can cash them in later when the challenges of life get a little more complicated for your kids.

What about you?

Use your gift of genius before they realize that it's really just experience. Be your child's teacher. This summer, take your kid to a ball game and teach him or her to fill out a scorecard.

GREAT AND UNEXPECTED THINGS

"It is a wise father that knows his own child."

William Shakespeare

If you ask most kids what they want to be when they grow up, they'll give you an expected answer. The little ones want to be ballerinas, caped crusaders, and sports stars. The older ones want to be something a little more practical. My experience tells me that most maturing kids have one or two secret ambitions they won't tell anyone but their closest friends. It could be a secret dream they've had for years or a recent self-discovery. Your fifth-grader may come across a vicarious career choice in a book or movie, but they're too timid to share that dream. Your high-schooler may be considering an unconventional college major or career and is afraid to speak it out loud because of what family and friends might say.

Dad, if you can somehow figure out that secret ambition and nurture it, you will gain new hero status. Don't interrogate them. Don't read their diary. Be more subtle. Make note of what they're reading, what they write about in English class, and the private conversations happening in the backseat of your SUV.

Open the door to their secret dreams and watch them do great and unexpected things. They'll thank you every day for the rest of their lives.

What about you?

Do you have any secret ambitions? It's not too late. It's a wise man who knows himself.

ROCK MUSIC

"Sing a new song to the LORD! Sing his praises from the ends of the earth!"

ISAIAH 42:10 NLT

For the first time in public, I present the lyrics to five songs I wrote during five highly emotional periods of my life.

These words have never been written down until now. And never heard outside the walls of my home (other than in a maternity ward). Except for the first one, these songs were all written on the days my kids were born. Alec's song was written two days after his birth as I rocked him at the neonatal intensive-care unit at Lutheran General Hospital. I remember it like it was yesterday.

Alec, Alec, my little pal.
Alec, Alec, I love you so.
© 1980 Jay K. Payleitner

Randy, Randy, Randy, you're my boy.
Randy, Randy, my pride and joy.
© 1983 Jay K. Payleitner

Max, Max, it's a fact.
You're my guy. You're my...Max!
© 1986 Jay K. Payleitner

Isaac, Isaac, God smiled.
On my son, Isaac Jay.
© 1988 Jay K. Payleitner

Rae Anne, Rae Anne, ray of sunshine.
My little girl, brightens each day.
© 1993 Jay K. Payleitner

Gentlemen, don't let Mom be the only one to sing lullabies to your babies. And don't sweat it if you can't come up with a personal song for each of your kids, although it doesn't have to be a Grammy-winning tune. Just sing your favorite rock song, hymn, or TV theme song, as long as it's sung with a smile and gentle voice. But I must say, melodically whispering your newborn's name as you hold them close is a great way to start a life and a relationship.

To Alec, Randall, Max, Isaac, and Rae Anne: Sorry, the secret's out. Your song—written for your ears only—is now immortalized in this devotional for dads everywhere. But really, only the lyrics are public. The tune is still in my head. And yours.

What about you?

Even if you can't carry a tune in a bucket, your kids should know your singing voice. From lullabies to worship songs to the national anthem, music is a heartfelt way to connect with your kids and bring your family together.

FIRM GRIP. EYE CONTACT. HEAD NOD.

"Peace I leave with you; my peace I give you. I do not give to you as the world gives. Do not let your hearts be troubled and do not be afraid."

John 14:27

In the early part of your church service, are you given a chance to shake hands with the people around you? Some churches call it "the sign of peace."

How do your kids do with that? It's actually a pretty good time to make sure they know how to shake hands and show respect to their elders. It's also a time when you can model all kinds of positive behavior. Non-silly handshakes. Eye contact. Inside voices. Polite smiles. Personal boundaries. How to meet new people. How to greet old friends. All in 20 seconds or less!

Of course, you model those things in the moment. The teaching can come before or after the service. It's not a lecture, it's a teachable moment. Say something like, "What do you think of shaking hands during the service?" Whatever their response, honor it and add to it. If you see them getting silly or awkward in their handshaking, go ahead and practice.

Shaking hands is a life skill. Dad, that's one you can teach!

What about you?

So many life skills are learned by watching Dad do it. Often, the skill is practiced in public, but any follow-up teaching should happen in private.

TRUSTING TRADITIONS

"What an enormous magnifier is tradition! How a thing grows in the human memory and in the human imagination, when love, worship, and all that lies in the human heart, is there to encourage it."

THOMAS CARLYLE

Chances are your family has dozens of traditions. You may not call them such, but that's what they are, and they are enormously important to your kids.

Stopping for ice cream during bike rides. Sitting in the same pew at church. Ordering Extra Crispy rather than Original Recipe at KFC. Visiting the zoo every summer. Toasting with hot chocolate every New Year's Eve. Stopping by Nana's gravestone on her birthday. Making s'mores in the fireplace. Posing for photos on the first day of school.

Traditions make a family. And Dad, I recommend you crown yourself "Official Keeper of Traditions." If you accept that role, you'll establish yourself as trustworthy and consistent. Your children will honor you and follow your instruction because they have come to rely on you day after day, year after year.

One of the expectations of church elders, outlined in 1 Timothy 3:4, is that an elder "must manage his own family well, having children who respect and obey him" (NLT). Keeping traditions is a part of managing your family and raising children who are on the same page as you—respectful and obedient.

What about you?

Surprising your kids with new treats and adventures is a totally cool thing for dads to do. But consistency and tradition-keeping needs to be the standard that makes surprises all the more delightful. Fathering without traditions is like playing a game without any rules.

WORKING IT OUT

"One hundred religious persons knit into a unity by careful organization do not constitute a church any more than eleven dead men make a football team. The first requisite is life, always."

A.W. Tozer

I hope this idea doesn't take you by surprise. Men, we can no longer just take our kids to church and hope it rubs off on them.

Our children need proof that salvation is worth the effort and that God is worthy of our devotion. They need to see an authentic Christian faith that's making a real difference in a real person's life. Dad, you're nominated.

What's the plan? Start by letting them observe you seeking God's will and applying God's truth to your daily challenges. Let them see how God works in your life. With wisdom, you may even need to share stories of how you've struggled with sin and its sordid repercussions. Make sure to finish each disclosure with the confirmation that only through Christ did you find rescue and healing.

This is what Paul was talking about when he wrote,

> *Continue to work out your salvation with fear and trembling, for it is God who works in you to*

will and to act in order to fulfill his good purpose (Philippians 2:12-13).

Just to clarify. Paul wasn't telling the Philippians to work *for* their salvation. That work has already been done on the cross. He was saying to work *out* your salvation. To put your faith into action. To allow God to work in and through you.

If your faith is something you just wear, your kids will not be impressed. But if your faith is something that works, it will leave quite an impression.

What about you?

You have a story that needs to be told. A before-and-after story of your life before and after Christ. Don't make something up. But do paint a dramatic word picture of how Jesus has changed your life. Practice sharing it with a friend. Then share it with your kids.

DOGS, YES—MOSQUITOES, NO

"To pretend to describe the excellence, the greatness or duration of the happiness of heaven by the most artful composition of words would be but to darken and cloud it; to talk of raptures and ecstasies, joy and singing, is but to set forth very low."

JONATHAN EDWARDS

Daddy, what's heaven like?"

"Do dogs go to heaven?"

"Dad, heaven sounds boring. What will I do for eternity?"

Hollywood has imagined it. Books have been written on it. And dads continue to be stumped by questions about it.

When my kids asked me if something, someone, or some pet would be in heaven, I used to say, "God will make sure you will be perfectly happy there. If he thinks you need banana splits or our golden retriever, Madison, to be happy, then you can count on it."

Theologians might not approve 100 percent of that idea of heaven, but I don't think I'm far off. Even the Bible uses metaphors, hyperbole, and earthly imagery to describe heaven. Streets paved with gold? A crystal sea? A place with many mansions? I am not taking any of that literally.

I do know that heaven will have no moths, rust, or thieves to destroy or steal my stuff (Matthew 6:20). But that doesn't really matter because *we won't have any stuff.* I'm mostly hoping there will be no mosquitoes.

When your kids ask you (and I hope they do) it may be wisest to quote or paraphrase what Paul wrote to the Corinthians: "No eye has seen, no ear has heard, and no mind has imagined what God has prepared for those who love him" (1 Corinthians 2:9 NLT).

What about you?

Got your mansion reserved? I do. Tell your children often that you look forward to hanging out with them for eternity.

PREPARED IN ADVANCE

"We are God's handiwork, created in Christ Jesus to do good works, which God prepared in advance for us to do."

EPHESIANS 2:10

For the first 12 to 14 years of life, I believe you should regularly tell each of your kids, "Son…daughter…you can do anything you set your mind to." That kind of statement helps them see the unlimited nature of the universe and challenges them to consider the many options they have to serve the Creator of that universe.

But as the high-school years approach, you'll want to change your encouragement strategy. About that time, they begin to realize they cannot literally do anything they set their mind to. Doors start to close. And that's okay. Young teens are the ones doing the closing. At that age, my daughter knew she was not going to be the next Monet. At that age, my older son knew he wasn't going to be the next Frank Lloyd Wright. At that age, self-aware kids begin to realize they're just not cut out for certain careers.

All of this means they are beginning to discern their true gifts and abilities. And Dad, that's when you can turn to a wonderful passage of Scripture that calls them to identify those gifts and commit to them with diligence and excellence.

> *We have different gifts, according to the grace given to each of us. If your gift is prophesying, then prophesy in accordance with your faith; if it is serving, then serve; if it is teaching, then teach; if it is to encourage, then give encouragement; if it is giving, then give generously; if it is to lead, do it diligently; if it is to show mercy, do it cheerfully (Romans 12:6-8).*

That's also when you can start saying, "Son... daughter...I can't wait to see how God uses your gift of (fill in the blank)."

What about you?

The promise found in this verse from Romans is quite useful for those seasons when your child is feeling giftless. The first four words confirm that "we have different gifts." Dad, it can be quite a fulfilling adventure for a father to join his child as they try new things and explore new worlds in that quest to identify their unique and valuable gifts.

GUYS BEHAVING MANLY

"Sing for joy to God our strength."

Psalm 81:1

Have you ever experienced worship surrounded only by other baritone voices booming off the walls with no annoying chirpy sopranos to distract you? It's more powerful than any scene from *Gladiator* or *300.*

Whether it's through Promise Keepers, Iron Sharpens Iron, Man in the Mirror, or a church men's ministry-sponsored event, I am quite certain that men meeting with men is a powerful tool for sharing biblical truth, holding each other accountable, and learning to be better husbands and fathers. The worship proves that point.

Way back in 1996, I took my two oldest sons to Soldier Field in Chicago for a Promise Keepers event. When a stadium of guys sings "Our God Is an Awesome God," you can't help but believe it. I still wonder if any cars driving by on Lake Shore Drive felt the power that day. When we sang "Lord, I Lift Your Name on High," his name was indeed lifted higher than any of the buildings in the backdrop of the Chicago skyline.

It's undeniably emotional. But don't get me wrong, the worship I'm talking about is not a superficial moment driven by volume and group dynamics. This is about knowing who we are and knowing who God is. It is simultaneously surrender and empowerment. It is admitting we have many questions but knowing we serve a God with all the answers. It's trusting that even though we don't know what tomorrow will bring, we can trust him for an eternity of days. That's why he is awesome. That's why we lift up his name.

What about you?

In the next few months, seek out a men's ministry conference. Take your son, age 6, 60, or in between.

FROM PROTECTING TO PREPARING

"You know your children are growing up when they stop asking you where they came from and refuse to tell you where they're going."

P.J. O'Rourke (1947–)

Kids are supposed to grow, be curious, discover new things, and test your boundaries. That's their job.

Your job is to keep open lines of communication, set a good example, enter their world, give reasonable warnings, rescue them, love them, and pray for them.

A generation or two ago, parents could shield their kids from most of the cruddiest crud of the world. But that's just not possible anymore. Laptops and tablets go everywhere and reveal everything. The media has turned from your advocate to your enemy. Neighbors on the same block no longer agree about right and wrong. Up until a few years ago, school boards could take a stand against clearly immoral choices and values. Today, trends such as social justice, cultural diversity, and "alternative lifestyle education" ensure that your child will be indoctrinated with falsehoods masquerading as truth.

The best way to protect them is to prepare them.

Your innocent, wide-eyed seven-year-old son or daughter is about to get blasted by a culture that has no moral compass. Your teenager is already surrounded and in desperate need of reinforcements. It's a good thing you're there, Dad, to guide them through the darkness into light.

What about you?

Kids are still kids. They walk without fear into the shadows. Unfortunately, the stakes are higher and the shadows are deeper and darker than ever. Don't give up, Dad. You are your child's most important protector.

A VERSE THAT'S TOUGH TO SWALLOW

"Fathers, do not embitter your children, or they will become discouraged."

Colossians 3:21

I hate this verse. I hate to think about parents who leave their children with a bitter taste—joyless, resentful. I hate the idea of kids—young lives with great potential—giving up and just not caring anymore. I hate to consider that I may have brought a measure of discouragement to one or more of my children.

It's pretty easy to do. We slide a clever sarcastic remark across the dinner table. We chastise our kids for behavior we've been modeling for years. We set expectations that are beyond their capabilities or far different from their hopes and dreams. We make a correction and then make it again, again, and again without giving them time to process it. We degrade them in front of their friends.

And here's a thought by which I've been convicted. Through extra effort and determination your child makes an improvement in a field of study, athletics, creative arts, or other worthwhile pursuit. Instead of congratulating or celebrating, you give off a vibe or even use words that say, "It's about time" or "Of course—I would expect nothing less."

Often, when we're trying to do the right thing as fathers is exactly when we push too hard or say too much.

As with so many biblical admonitions, it's helpful to turn this one upside down. Allow me to paraphrase. "Dads, speak encouragement to kids and allow them to chase their dreams and they will become courageous and empowered."

What about you?

I'm pro-dad. The last thing I want to do is make any father feel cruddy or filled with regrets. But Colossians 3:21 is part of the Good Book. So in a book of devotions for dads, we really did need to take a look at that verse. Right?

WE DON'T NEED NO STINKIN' RULES

"If you obey all the rules you miss all the fun."

Katherine Hepburn

If we ask a bunch of five-year-olds what they think of rules, we have a pretty good idea how they will respond. Rules are no fun. Having rules means there are things you can't do. Rules get in the way. But as they get older—if they have parents, teachers, and coaches who love them—those same kids will discover that rules create crucial and helpful boundaries, organization, and foundations. Learn the rules of science and you make new discoveries. Learn the proper technique for glassblowing, throwing pots, or welding and you can sculpt evocative pieces of art. Learn how chess pieces move and you can advance beyond checkers. Learn how to throw a knuckle curve, slider, and changeup and the scouts will show up at your high-school diamond.

Without rules, chaos reigns. Without rules every inventor, artist, scholar, or athlete would have to start from square one. There would be no record of past achievement. Without rules you wouldn't know whether you had done something that had never been done before. Without rules, we couldn't keep score.

(And then how would we know who won on *Monday Night Football*?)

In his second letter to Timothy, Paul makes an excellent case for following rules. "Athletes cannot win the prize unless they follow the rules" (2 Timothy 2:5 NLT).

What about you?

It's not just kindergarten kids who have trouble with rules. Sure, most kids get the hang of rules in grade school. But sometime later they have to do one last season of testing the rules—your rules. It may be a few days in middle school. It may be a summer hanging out with the wrong crowd in high school. It may be three semesters in college. It may be the entire decade of their twenties. Your children will surely spend a season of life wrestling with rules. See if you can be close by to catch them before they land too hard and break themselves into a million pieces.

TENSION IN THE AIR

"Words from the mouth of a wise man are gracious, while the lips of a fool consume him."

ECCLESIASTES 10:12 NASB

If you're in that stage of life during which kids are constantly underfoot, you may not fully appreciate this concept. But sometime in the future, you will miss having your kids around. Really.

During their teen years they will choose to spend time someplace other than your home. That includes the basement, the backyard, or the lakeside cottage of a high-school friend. Youth retreats, sports camps, and mission trips. College visits, slumber parties, and weekends with out-of-state cousins. You'll want to confirm that all these events have responsible adult supervision, but there's no reason to feel like you're being abandoned. It's good for teens to leave the nest once in a while on a trial run.

Around that time, some parents begin to experience a different kind of distance. It's not just physical separation. It's emotional. Or even spiritual.

If you are seeing less and less of your maturing teen, don't panic, but do listen to your own heart. Is your son or daughter missing family functions they once enjoyed? During the times they are home is the air filled with tension and terse words? Don't make accusations or point fingers. Instead, admit that something is in the way. With their busy lives, it's easy for kids to continue to the next stage of life as if nothing is amiss. So, Dad, it's up to you to take the initiative, pick up the phone, and say, "Hey, I miss you. Can I buy you lunch sometime next week?" Or something like that.

Is that something you need to do? Find the words, then make the call or send the text.

What about you?

Most of the time when you and your son or daughter are miscommunicating, the earlier you can get back on track, the easier it is. Still, even if it's been awhile and even if it feels awkward, don't give up. The cohesiveness of your family is too important.

HERITAGE VS. LEGACY

"If there is anything that we wish to change in our children, we should first examine it and see whether it is not something that could better be changed in ourselves."

CARL JUNG

Consider your parents. For better or worse, they have made an indelible impression on your mind and heart. They have left you with all kinds of attitudes, opinions, virtues, and vices. Some good. Some not so good. You need to ask yourself and decide, *What am I going to hang onto? What am I going to cast aside?*

Hint: Keep things like integrity, generosity, gratitude, gentleness, respect, diligence, and love. Rid yourself of things like laziness, rage, envy, racism, spite, faultfinding, and vulgarity.

In the process of doing this attribute analysis, you may think that you are turning your back on your parents, dishonoring them. In truth, they want you to achieve more, love more, and make fewer mistakes than they did. The best way to honor them—the fifth commandment—is to live your life at the highest level of excellence and connection to your Creator. Isn't that what you want for your children?

So look at your family history, learn from it, take

the best, and chuck the rest. The past, present, and future come together at this unique point in time. Don't miss it.

Your heritage has been defined by others. It has limits and liabilities. But your legacy remains undefined. It has no limits. It only has potential.

What about you?

What attitudes, attributes, and worldview have you kept from your own father? What have you intentionally set aside? Okay. Now, what do you want your children to keep or cast away from what you are leaving them? Okay. What if you cast away all your bad stuff today?

ACKNOWLEDGING SIN

"Love covers a multitude of sins."

1 Peter 4:8 NASB

We mess up. At least I do. And I have a sneaking suspicion you do too. The chance for men in our culture to fall into a puddle, pool, or ocean of sin is 100 percent. A cursory review of the seven deadly sins is enough to convict us and remind us that we are far, far, far from perfect. For the record, we're looking at greed, sloth, envy, wrath, pride, lust, or gluttony. When you sift through that list, I'm not sure which one you park on, but "pride" tends to bust my chops more and more these days. The other six aren't far behind.

Thankfully, love covers not just seven sins, but a multitude of sins. That verse in 1 Peter is referring to God's grace. The idea is that God knows us and loves us. He knows our shortcomings and imperfections. He even expects them. Yes, he's disappointed in our sins. They break his heart. But still, nothing we do can ever separate us from his perfect love.

Is there a lesson in there someplace for dads? Probably several.

For ourselves: Acknowledge our own sinful condition. Flee the world's carnality. Ask God consistently and constantly for help. Be broken before him, knowing you can rest in his grace.

For our kids: As fathers, we need to allow our own love to cover a multitude of our children's sins. Let's strive to know and understand what our kids are going through. Expect them to make mistakes. Be disappointed sometimes. But never let anything get in the way of your unconditional love.

Those sins/mistakes/flubs/screwups often come with repercussions. Love doesn't necessarily cover those. We and our kids often have to pay the penalty for our sins here on earth. But in the long run—in eternity—it all works out for good to those who are called according to God's purpose.

What about you?

Who are you tougher on—your kids or yourself? Maybe it's time to really get serious and lead your family to a life of brokenness, surrender, and new life in Christ. On the other hand, maybe it's time to take three steps back and cut yourself and your kids some slack. Grace rocks.

EVERY KID DESERVES A BLESSING

"A voice from heaven said, 'This is my Son, whom I love; with him I am well pleased.'"

MATTHEW 3:17

A Father gives a blessing to his Son. Thus launching a three-year ministry that ends with the most important event in the history of the world. That's powerful stuff.

Did your father give you a blessing? Did he tell you he loved you and was well-pleased with you? Did he do it in front of others, giving it even greater weight and authority? If not, don't you wish he had?

Can you take a hint, Dad?

Do this with each of your kids. Bless them. Officially tell them you love them. Officially tell them you are well-pleased with them.

That blessing can take all kinds of forms. It could be a one-time event with grand hoopla on their thirteenth birthday surrounded by dozens of family members. Or you could purposefully pray over each child every fall as you send them back to school. Or simply say a prayer of blessing every night when you tuck them in.

You could create a "rite of passage" ceremony to

mark their entry into adulthood and adult responsibility. You may want to present them with a symbolic gift to mark the occasion: a ring, a Bible, a sword, a necklace, a letter, a set of car keys, a pony.

Whatever way you choose to deliver your blessing it should follow the model of Matthew 3:17. Make sure it is audible, includes the word *love*, and expresses the idea that you are glad you are their father and they are your child.

What about you?

Here's an interesting observation about that blessing from God to his Son. Jesus had not yet begun his earthly ministry. Still God was "well pleased" with his Son. Is it possible we could tell our sons and daughters we are proud of them even when they haven't done something awesome recently?

HOME IS WHERE YOUR HEART IS

"When everything is ready, I will come and get you, so that you will always be with me where I am."

Jesus, speaking in John 14:3 NLT

Here's a story to tell your kids. And yourself.

A hundred years ago, a gray-haired couple is returning from overseas after a lifetime of mission work. As they begin to walk down the gangplank from the ocean liner, they are pleasantly surprised to see a brass band and a small crowd cheering their arrival. The wife turns to her husband and says, "Look, my dear. After all these years, the body of Christ is honoring us for our work."

But as they step onto the wharf, it becomes immediately clear to the couple that the attention of the revelers is directed beyond them to the ship's railing. They turn to see Teddy Roosevelt waving from the deck of the ship. The former president and his entourage whisk off to their busy, important lives leaving the missionary couple with three worn suitcases, a tattered steamer trunk, and two broken hearts.

With an unexpected touch of anger, the husband mutters, "After all we've sacrificed and four decades of service, is it too much to ask that someone have the decency to welcome us home?" In that moment a voice speaks gently from the sky: "My child, you're not home yet."

Where's your heart? Are you and your family living for here? Or living for heaven? These four words are a pretty good reminder for any time we don't get what we want. And also when we do! "We're not home yet."

What about you?

Should hard work and grand effort on behalf of the kingdom be applauded? Absolutely. But if that's your motivation, you're doing it for the wrong reason. Remind your children often that God sees what you're doing even when no one else is watching. Read Matthew, chapter 6, with your kids about giving and praying in secret. Plus, that chapter includes the Lord's Prayer!

MILE MARKER 12:1

"Let us run with perseverance the race marked out for us."

HEBREWS 12:1

You may think this verse is about endurance. And you wouldn't be wrong. We can all certainly imagine this verse on a poster featuring some lean-muscled cross-country runner pounding pavement, sweat trickling down the side of his face.

But did you ever consider the second half of this verse? Is there really a predetermined race course? Who marks it out? And is it just for us?

Yes, perseverance is important. Endurance. Follow-through. Striving to reach the goal. But more important—job one—is to identify the *right* goal. You certainly don't want to run with perseverance toward the wrong goal.

When it comes to our children, Dads, our primary task may be to help them identify their gifts and talents. Pray long and hard for them and with them about what God's plan is for their life. Establish some markers along the way—short- and long-term goals. Point the way—maybe even running alongside them for the first few miles—and then let them leave you in the dust.

That's a good thing. Because that particular race isn't marked out for you, it's marked out for them.

What about you?

You know all those Bible verses rumbling around in your head? Pull a few of them out and see if there is a phrase or two you've been overlooking.

DON'T MISS THE GLORY

"Parents are often so busy with the physical rearing of children that they miss the glory of parenthood, just as the grandeur of the trees is lost when raking leaves."

MARCELENE COX

Hey, new dad! Are you up to your knees in dirty diapers, baby bottles, and stained bibs, with a young wife mired in postpartum depression?

Hey, hardworking father of sprouting children! Are you trying to build a career while also being a model parent—feigning interest at back-to-school night, scratching your head over math homework, dramatizing bedtime stories, and racing to the office-supply store before it closes for poster board and markers?

Hey, dad of a teenager! Are you tossing car keys across the kitchen, bending curfews, opening your home to mobs of voracious adolescents, worrying about teen sex, and thinking about how you're ever going to pay for college?

In the midst of the nonstop labor, please don't miss the glory of parenthood.

When you and your family are diligently raking leaves, it's essential to stop and take in the crisp air, autumn colors, and the honking geese as they V overhead. That's glory.

One evening, when you pause to see your son and a friend playing Scrabble, your daughter noodling on the piano, your older boy finishing his algebra homework at the kitchen table, and your wife reading in her favorite chair—that's glory.

Watch for it, Dad, and your children will provide you with unexpected moments of shared laughter, surprising generosity, newly discovered giftedness, sudden spiritual insights, wisdom beyond their years, and hugs for no reason at all.

That's glory. Don't miss it.

What about you?

Look for moments of glory in your own private world. They may be small, but they can make all the difference in your day. And your life.

ONE OUT OF SEVEN

"Remember the sabbath day, to keep it holy."

Exodus 20:8 NASB

Is Sunday getting to be just like any other day with your family? Sure, you hustle off to church in the morning, but after that it's every man for himself. Maybe it's become a convenient day to run to the mall or grocery store. To pay bills. Catch up on some work. Hunker down with your computer. For many families, Sunday is the busiest traveling-sports day of the week, with tournaments from dawn to dusk.

I don't mind that some of the Old Testament mandates are not really emphasized anymore. A little work on Sunday is probably okay. Raking leaves or washing the car with your eight-year-old might be the exactly right pleasant way to spend the afternoon. Proofreading your teenager's term paper that's due the next day is "work," but it's not labor for an employer outside the home. Still, you have to agree that we've lost some of the simple charms of what Sunday could and should be. Family time. Drinking lemonade on the porch. Picnics. Sunday drives out into the country. Dare I suggest that Sundays might be set aside for some spiritual reflection or family devotions?

I confess that Sunday evenings often find me planning my upcoming workweek. Really, that's the exact time I should be investing in my family and helping them plan not just a week, but their lives.

What about you?

Honoring the Sabbath is one of the Ten Commandments. (And those are still in force, by the way.) What are you doing this weekend to keep holy the Lord's day?

COMMIT—THEN WATCH WHAT HAPPENS

"The moment one definitely commits oneself, then Providence moves too. All sorts of things occur to help one that would never otherwise have occurred. A whole stream of events issue from the decision, raising in one's favor all manner of unforeseen incidents and meetings and material assistance which no man could have dreamed would have come his way."

W.H. Murray

We need to get our kids to understand this big idea. Don't wait until the stars align perfectly to follow God's call on your life. Instead, take a bold first step and trust that God will direct a thousand more steps down a path chosen just for you. Along the way he may take you through dark tunnels and along thorny paths. But he will also give you courage, strength, and wisdom exactly when you need it. He will open hidden gates, provide unexpected resources, and introduce you to gifted strangers who will become best friends along the way.

The quote suggests that God moves. We know that's not true. He is an unshakable rock, a firm foundation. But when one of our kids (or one of us) commits our life journey to him, God's heart is indeed moved. His strength overflows into that new disciple. He promises to empower those who make a conscious decision to step out in faith. Second Chronicles 16:9 tells us that "the eyes of the LORD range throughout the earth to strengthen those whose hearts are fully committed to him."

Wouldn't you eagerly accept that new surge of strength for yourself? And for your children?

What about you?

Commit yourself to something that's beyond you. Help your kids do the same.

I THOUGHT I WAS WRONG ONCE, BUT I WAS MISTAKEN

"The people who think they know everything are a great annoyance to those of us who do."

Isaac Asimov

Don't know about you, but I'm right much more often than I'm wrong. At least I think so. Although, I could be wrong.

With that confession, let me turn to a turning point in your child's life you may not be aware of. It's when they move from "Dad knows everything" to "Dad doesn't know what he's talking about." Not coincidentally, that comes right around the middle-school years.

Don't panic, Dad. Yes, it's fun being the guy who already has all the answers. But it can be even more fulfilling to be the guy your son or daughter comes to when seeking a partner in finding answers and making new discoveries.

Even better than a know-it-all dad is a dad who models humility, curiosity, and a desire to learn. Want your kids to really honor you? Check out Proverbs 29:23: "A man's pride will bring him low, but a humble spirit will obtain honor" (NASB).

What about you?

Can you admit to your kids that you're not perfect? FYI—you're not, so you should.

THE CIRCLE GAME

"You don't really understand human nature unless you know why a child on a merry-go-round will wave at his parents every time around— and why his parents will always wave back."

WILLIAM D. TAMMEUS

I love the image in the quote above. It's a snapshot of kids growing up and parents letting go.

The child does something daring. In this case, it's straddling a painted pony and enduring a cacophony of garish colors and noise. They're no longer holding onto Dad's strong hand or Mom's secure apron strings. Suddenly, they are whooshed out of sight. They're gone. On their own.

But what happens on each revolution? As they come full circle, they look for you and loosen their grip with one hand just long enough to wave with delight.

The only reason a small child has such courage is because they know you will be there just in case they need to be rescued. Seeing you standing firm at every revolution provides the exact security they need. And it confirms the heart connection you need. The exuberant wave is not hello or goodbye—it's saying, "We're in this together."

Remember the carousel.

Embrace that image when your children do anything daring. Kindergarten. Their first date. Their first job. College. The mission field. The military. Be there to send them off and welcome them back. And stand firm every minute in between.

What about you?

Imagine a dad at a carousel who's suddenly not there. That's what happens when a family splits up. Don't let that loss of foundation happen to your kids.

WIN EVERY DEBATE

"Be sure you put your feet in the right place, then stand firm."

ABRAHAM LINCOLN

Members of a high-school debate team sometimes take part in an exercise that seems impossible to me. They draw a controversial issue out of a hat and are instructed to take one side of that issue and develop arguments based on logic and reason.

My response is... "Arrrggghh!" What if my slip of paper dictates I take the wrong side of the debate? I don't think I would want to give voice to arguments for abortion rights, lowering the drinking age, or removing the words "under God" from the Pledge of Allegiance. On the other hand, one of the important strategies in debate is to know both sides of the issue. You don't need to agree, but you do need to know what the opposition believes and why they feel that way. If I can understand and anticipate the position of my opponents, then I can strengthen my own arguments.

Especially as your kids get older, don't just tell them what to believe. Tell them why. Help them choose where to stand and equip them to stand firm on their own.

What about you?

Memorize 1 Peter 3:15: "Always be prepared to give an answer to everyone who asks you to give the reason for the hope that you have. But do this with gentleness and respect."

GOD WILL NOT BE MOCKED

"God will pardon me. It's his job."

HEINRICH HEINE (1797–1856)

Heinrich Heine was a talented poet and journalist of nineteenth-century Germany. But he was also a bit of a scoundrel. The government banished him, and he twice had to defend himself in duels. He lay paralyzed for much of the last decade of his life without complaint and gained some public sympathy. As the story goes, on his deathbed, when asked if he had gotten right with the Lord, he replied, "God will pardon me. It's his job."

Some may interpret that as a refreshing and accurate description of grace. God does love the world. He did choose to send his Son to pay for our sins so we might be pardoned. But I'm not comfortable enough to say that's God's job.

On the other hand, because there is no hint of brokenness in Mr. Heine's words, I am assuming that he was unrepentant and was, in fact, mocking the Creator of the universe. As an educated man, Heinrich Heine should have known better. When he died in 1856, Bibles were readily available to the public, and he very likely had come across the clear New Testament passage, "Do not be deceived: God cannot be mocked. A man reaps what he sows" (Galatians 6:7).

What about you?

Your kids are watching. Do you show respect for God, his Word, and his church? Are you living in a healthy fear of the Lord? Or do you find yourself taking God for granted? Whatever you are planting in the hearts and minds of your kids, that's what they are going to reap as they mature.

DADDY, TELL ME A STORY

"From childhood you have known the Holy Scriptures, which are able to make you wise for salvation through faith which is in Christ Jesus."

2 Timothy 3:15 NKJV

Have you mastered the art of telling bedtime stories? Whether you're reading a classic Dr. Seuss story or pulling a fairy tale from your own imagination, there are several strategies for getting the most out of it. Get close and comfy. Use silly voices and sound effects. If you're reading a story to the younger kids, invite the older ones. Ten-year-olds may not admit it, but they still love bedtime stories.

Make wise use of resources from your local Christian bookstore. Bible storybooks that appeal to children have come a long way in recent years.

Don't hesitate to pull out your own Bible. Even in "grown-up" Bibles, there are captivating stories—actual events—that kids can totally understand. "Who made the world?" (Genesis 1). "The giant boat" (Genesis 6 and 7). "The man the lions wouldn't eat" (Daniel 6). "Three guys in a furnace" (Daniel 3). "The lost boy found at church" (Luke 2:41-52). "Short guy up a tree" (Luke 19).

Don't forget to make good use of the parables of

Jesus and follow his secret to delivering the moral of the story. Jesus doesn't just recite a lesson—he leads the audience to their own conclusion.

For example, after sharing the story we now call "The Good Samaritan," Jesus asked, "Which of these three do you think proved to be a neighbor to the man who fell into the robbers' hands?" When his audience gave him the obvious answer, Jesus gave an equally obvious—but necessary—command, "Yes, now go and do the same."

What about you?

The Bible doesn't change lives. God changes lives when people apply the truths of the Bible. (And by the way, this book also doesn't do squat unless you apply what you're learning.)

TURN RIGHT AT THE NEXT INTERSECTION

"Your ears will hear a word behind you, 'This is the way, walk in it,' whenever you turn to the right or to the left."

ISAIAH 30:21 NASB

I love that God doesn't just wind us up and turn us loose.

We can be confident in our relationship with him. We can have a clear plan for our life. We can develop a good set of biblical values based on clear principles such as integrity, respect for life, honesty, kindness, self-control, and more. But still, sometimes we come to a crossroads and don't know which way to go.

We don't have to be like the Scarecrow, pointing every which way when Dorothy asks directions to the Emerald City. All we have to do is listen. God will tell us. If we listen carefully we should even be able to identify that voice as the Holy Spirit.

When you explain this principle to your kids, don't be surprised if they say, "That's kind of like GPS on my smartphone." Well, yeah, I guess. Sort of. One difference is that God's voice doesn't sound exasperated when he says, "Recalculating."

What about you?

Looking for the Way? Just to remind you, in John 14:6 Jesus confirms that he is the way, the truth, and the life.

IN WEAKNESS, STRENGTH

"He said to me, 'My grace is sufficient for you, for my power is made perfect in weakness.' Therefore I will boast all the more gladly about my weaknesses, so that Christ's power may rest on me."

2 Corinthians 12:9

You can spend a lot of time telling your kids how great they are. But somewhere along the line they are going to realize they have shortcomings. Other kids are brighter, cuter, stronger, taller, or faster. They are going to come to grips with a personal character trait or physical challenge that the world would call a weakness. They may be shy, clumsy, tongue-tied, or prone to ramble with their words. They may be a sore loser or an overachiever. They may have trouble concentrating on tedious tasks or taking orders from authority figures.

Whatever their affliction, be ready with this verse. When they finally come to you with regrets and frustrations about who they are and how God made them, just smile and open your Bible to 2 Corinthians 12:5-10. Tell them you already know all about that personality quirk of theirs and you love them anyway!

Tell them everyone has at least one flaw. Or two. Or

more. Then tell them about Paul's unidentified "thorn in the flesh." Explain how the apostle was grateful for his affliction.

Be wise here, Dad. Don't diminish your child's fears or frustrations. Love them in and through this life-changing lesson. And don't forget to finish with that great line from the end of the passage: "When I am weak, then I am strong."

What about you?

What's your "thorn in the flesh"? What's your defining weakness? Even as you open your Bible to share lessons with your kids, don't forget to open your own life and share personal revelations God has given to you.

NOT A BAD WAY TO INVEST FOUR YEARS OF YOUR LIFE

"Drop out of school before your mind rots from exposure to our mediocre educational system."

FRANK ZAPPA (1940–1993)

What do these folks all have in common? Frank Lloyd Wright. Tom Hanks. Bill Gates. Tiger Woods. Buckminster Fuller. Steve Jobs. Lady Gaga. James Cameron. Harrison Ford. Mark Zuckerberg.

They are successful people (at least in the eyes of the world) who dropped out of college. Apparently a bachelor's degree is not necessary to pilot the *Millennium Falcon*, direct the computer-generated inhabitants of Pandora, or design Fallingwater. These famous names are listed here to prepare you for the time your son or daughter throws them in your face as proof that finishing college is not necessary.

Your response, Dad? Admit they have a point. But also point out that most of those famed individuals had a plan in place before dropping out. That can lead to some eye-opening follow-up questions of your own.

Questions like "What's your plan?" and "Where do you see yourself in ten years?"

Then finish your closing arguments with these figures from the U.S. Census Bureau: Workers 25 and over with a bachelor's degree earn an average yearly income of $60,594, while those with only a high-school diploma earn $33,618.*

What about you?

Never imply or say to your kids that money equals success. But what you can talk about is opportunity, listening to God's call in your life, and big-picture thinking. Be aware, Dad, that college also leads to new skills, new connections, and new ideas. (Which brings its own set of challenges for dads!)

---

* U.S. Census Bureau, 2008 report.

TEARING APART PROVERBS 22:6

"Train up a child in the way he should go, even when he is old he will not depart from it."

PROVERBS 22:6 NASB

This has to be the most frequently quoted parenting verse in the Bible. And it's jam-packed with great insight. Let's dissect it and see what it really says.

Proverbs 22:6 confirms that children can and should be trained. We don't let them wander recklessly through life doing whatever they think is right.

It suggests that each child is an individual. They have their own gifts and abilities given by the Creator. Which means that God has a reasonable customized plan for their life, a plan that makes perfect use of all they bring to the table.

It reveals that lessons learned early have staying power. So we need to start early and teach them eternal truths that have long-term value.

It reminds us that children grow older and leave the nest. We won't always be around to guide, rescue, or protect them. That's okay, because our training will stick with them.

The proverb also makes a promise. Do this and your

child will do that. It doesn't say "might" or "probably will" or "hopefully will." This 21-word proverb sounds cut and dried.

That puts the pressure on you, Dad. You are expected to train up each of your children in the way they should go. The fact that you picked up this book is a good indication you are up for that challenge.

What about you?

You can do this with any Bible verse. Break it down. Study each word and phrase. Apply it to your life. Go ahead—God's Word can stand up to your scrutiny.

LOSING AIN'T ALL BAD

"Failure is success if we learn from it."

Malcolm S. Forbes

I hate to sound like one of those Successories motivational posters, but the quotation above is absolutely true.

Watch what happens to the two teams after a close Little League or high-school baseball game. The teams jog out to right field and left field and everyone takes a knee. The winning team has a short meeting with lots of high fives and very little instruction. The losing coach goes quite a bit longer, pointing out skills that need improvement and beginning to strategize about which areas to work on for the next practice. You've seen it dozens of times.

But wait a second. Outfielders from both teams missed hitting the cutoff man. Batters from both dugouts missed signs, took some called third strikes, and failed to advance the runner in key situations.

If it was a close game, both teams probably made the same amount of mental and physical errors. That day, members of the losing team learned something after the game. The winners didn't. The next day, the losing coach is going to push his team a little harder—the winning coach may not.

It's no fun to lose. But I dare say, if the losing coach is getting the job done, the next time those two teams play, the result is going to be different.

Worth noting, Dad: After a disappointing performance, the last thing you want to do is throw a bunch of clichés at your kid. But the fact is that while it's fun to win, most improvement happens because next time you don't want to lose again.

What about you?

This lesson goes beyond sports, of course. As a matter of fact, Paul wrote to the Romans that we shouldn't simply endure setbacks, we should actually rejoice in them. "We can rejoice, too, when we run into problems and trials, for we know that they help us develop endurance" (Romans 5:3 NLT).

WHAT THE NEXT GENERATION SEES

"Each generation tells of your faithfulness to the next."
ISAIAH 38:19 NLT

You've heard the statistics.

- LifeWay Christian Resources reports that 75 percent of young people leave church in their late teens and do not later reconnect.
- Barna Research tells us "a majority of twenty-somethings—61 percent of today's young adults—had been churched at one point during their teen years but they are now spiritually disengaged."

Without getting bogged down in numbers and percentages, there is a real sense that young adults today do not see personal value in following the faith convictions of their moms and dads. They see little evidence that having a relationship with Jesus is worth the effort. The question worth asking is "Why?"

Fellow dads, I think it might be our fault.

Too often, our outward appearance does not reflect our dependence on God. When good things happen, we love to take the credit. When bad things happen, we fix it. In private, we might reveal our brokenness and need for a Savior. Behind closed doors, we will pray, seek wise spiritual counsel, and surrender, even tearfully, to God's will. But in public—the persona seen by our kids—we rarely acknowledge our need for God.

As a result, our children do not see how he has been working in us, for us, and through us.

What about you?

If your grown child steps away from church for a while, don't beat yourself up. Think back to spiritual turning points in their life. Did they ever sincerely turn their life over to Christ? Was there a solid season during which they were led by God's Spirit? Then keep praying, keep an open door, and trust that God will be faithful in drawing your child back to him. If your son or daughter has never accepted Christ as Savior, then pray even harder—pray for Christian peers and mentors to come into their life, and work to keep your family relationships strong. Badgering and harping won't help. Humbly letting them see God making a difference in your life will.

GOOD TIMES AND BAD

"Give thanks to the LORD, for he is good."

PSALM 107:1

There's a disconcerting habit spreading among well-intentioned Christians. When something good happens, they say, "God is good."

Does that sound right to you? It's absolutely true. When you get a flat tire in front of a Goodyear dealership, God is good. When the sun breaks through the clouds just as you're about to tee off at a course designed by Alister MacKenzie or Donald Ross, God is good. When your live-in mother-in-law gets invited to her sister's place in Boca for the winter, God is good.

But let me clarify something supremely important. When you get a flat tire in the middle of the desert, when your golf outing consists of nine third-graders on a course featuring green carpet, rusty gutters, and a windmill, and when your live-in mother-in-law adopts two poodles that are not house-trained, God is still good.

So I'm not suggesting you stop saying, "God is good." I am actually suggesting that you double the number of times you say it. In good times and bad.

Please note: Do not say it sarcastically in the same way that grown children living at home and working for minimum wage at Target might say, "I'm living the dream." Instead say it with a confident, trusting smile knowing that no matter what happens, God is going to take care of you in the long run.

What about you?

Next time something awesome happens in your life, let your children know that God provides. Next time something tragic happens in your life, let your children know that God still provides. The idea is—no matter what—to point to his faithfulness at all times in all things.

IT'S ALL HIS ANYWAY

"We make a living by what we get, we make a life by what we give."

SIR WINSTON CHURCHILL

Let's assume that you already buy into the idea of tithing—the idea of giving 10 percent of your income back to the Lord. The concept goes back to the Old Testament and is rooted in the fact that it's all God's anyway. We should be glad that he lets us keep the 90 percent!

> *Be sure to set aside a tenth of all that your fields produce each year (Deuteronomy 14:22).*

The question for today is, "When did you start tithing?" Very likely you were an adult and it took an eye-opening message and some real soul-searching. After a conversation with your wife, you decided together to begin giving sacrificially. Good for you! Since then, you have undoubtedly seen God's blessing pour into your lives in unexpected ways. Maybe not financially, but you've settled into a more contented life and gained some new freedoms. Tithing is a gift from God.

The real question today then is this: "When will you begin to encourage or challenge your own children to tithe?" With their summer jobs, babysitting and lawn-mowing money, and weekly allowance, shouldn't they be tithing so they can experience all the blessings of God's plan for our worldly wealth?

What about you?

If you're not tithing, start! If you are, tell your kids about how your sacrificial giving has helped you loosen your grip on worldly possessions.

GET THEM THINKING AND TALKING

"You don't have a soul. You are a Soul. You have a body."

C.S. Lewis

Is this idea from one of the greatest writers of the twentieth century too deep for your kids? I'll bet they can handle it. Maybe, Dad, it's too deep for you. So let's kick it around for a moment.

Here's what I'm thinking. A soul is what differentiates us from animals. When the Bible says we are created in the image of God, it doesn't mean that God has two arms, two legs, green eyes, and buckteeth. It means he has made us eternal beings capable of love, creativity, and rational thought. We are souls. At death, we will be separated from our bodies, but at Christ's return we will be reunited with a glorified body. What that body consists of is the topic of much debate. One last kick-around point. In this context, you can probably interchange the word *"spirit"* with *"soul"* without upsetting the scholars. The fact that you are a soul or spirit should not be confused with the Holy Spirit, the member of the Trinity who came to guide believers after Jesus' time on earth.

All that to say, now you are ready for that conversation with any of your kids age seven and above. Tell them, "You know that devotional for dads I'm reading? It quoted C.S. Lewis, and he said that humans are not bodies that have souls. Instead we are souls that have bodies. What do you think?"

What about you?

Do you avoid these kinds of conversations with your kids because you're not sure of what to say? You don't want to get it wrong? Well, step it up, man. Nobody has all the answers. Your kids need to see that it's healthy to talk about God and stuff. Dig in. Seek answers. Ask their opinion. Wrestling with spiritual truths with your kids can be a blast!

CATCH ANYTHING?

"Many men go fishing their entire lives without knowing it is not fish they are after."

HENRY DAVID THOREAU

After my dad died, I realized all the conversations I had not had with him. Questions regularly came to mind that now would never be answered. One question I had was whether he was disappointed that I had never found satisfaction in sitting in a rowboat for hours at a time waiting for a bluegill, crappie, or northern pike to tug on my line.

My dad enjoyed that. At least I think he did. For decades, every August the Payleitner family went "up north" with grandparents and extended family members to share in the traditions of catching, cleaning, and talking about fish. I didn't get it. I absolutely enjoyed the time with my dad and recall specific conversations and cherish the memories. But for this boy, a single hour on the water would have been enough. Four, not so much. Out of my teens, I never pursued the sport.

Not long ago, I asked my mom if it had made Dad sad that I had never become an avid fisherman. She looked at me quizzically and confirmed that it had never been an issue. Clearly, Dad had shared 50 years of experiences with me. Fishing was just one of many.

According to my mom, the fact that I didn't share that one hobby was nowhere near a concern. I was glad to hear it.

Still, I wish I had asked Dad that question.

What about you?

Is there anything left unsaid between you and your father? Something minuscule in importance? Something significant? Maybe…maybe, call him today.

PRODIGAL SON—I

"A few days later this younger son packed all his belongings and moved to a distant land, and there he wasted all his money in wild living."

LUKE 15:13 NLT

Theologians would say that Jesus' parable known as "The Prodigal Son" is about God's unconditional love and confirms that no matter what we've done, God will always celebrate the day when a lost person finally surrenders to grace. The younger son represents our sinful self. The father represents God. But I can't help but look at this famous parable as a lesson in family dynamics.

The bratty little brother demands big cash from Dad, who—for some reason—gives in. The kid blows the entire wad partying with strangers. But when the money is gone the friends don't stick around. Surprise, surprise. Every time I read what follows I think, *Boy, you are getting what you deserve—living with pigs.* But I'm still glad when the prodigal comes to his senses and heads home.

The lessons for a dad to point out to his teenage son or daughter are all over this parable in relation to the younger son: You can't buy friends. Don't trust in worldly things—they don't last. Hard work never hurt anyone, plus it gives you time to think. And of course,

"Dad loves you and will always welcome you with open arms."

Some may say that making your home a place of infinite, welcoming love creates a haven for freeloading boomerang kids. To the contrary. I suggest that your loving home leads to young adults having the desire to create their own loving homes and gives them a secure foundation and launching pad.

What about you?

Got a prodigal? If you have the courage, pray for your daughter or son to hit bottom. That may be the only way they finally realize their need for a Savior.

PRODIGAL SON—2

"While he was still a long way off, his father saw him coming. Filled with love and compassion, he ran to his son, embraced him, and kissed him."

Luke 15:20 NLT

Put yourself in this dad's shoes. Or sandals.

Your youngest son takes half your money and leaves town. You know he doesn't make good decisions. You know how tough the world is and that he's too young to make it on his own. You may have heard occasional reports about him from people traveling through his area. You know the famine has hit hard. Your boy—who you love so much—could very well be dead. Still, every day you stand for hours on the edge of your driveway hoping he'll return. You see a figure in the distance. It's skinny and threadbare, but you recognize him instantly. And you run to him.

Dad, is that how you would react if it happened to you? Is that how you will react when it does?

Maybe the main reason Luke included this parable is to remind fathers to be patient with their children. Dad, they are going to disappoint you. They may turn their back on you. They may squander your hard-earned money on "wild living." The example of the prodigal's father models just how vital it is to keep the door open. We may need to wait expectantly...for years.

When your prodigal child begins to take a few steps back toward you, you know what to do. Run to him. Run to her. And get ready to party.

What about you?

Does your prodigal know they can come home? You can't beg them. You can't make them. But you can let them know they are welcome in your home anytime with open arms...and an open refrigerator.

PRODIGAL SON—3

"The older brother was angry and wouldn't go in. His father came out and begged him, but he replied, 'All these years I've slaved for you and never once refused to do a single thing you told me to. And in all that time you never gave me even one young goat for a feast with my friends.'"

Luke 15:28-29 NLT

You cannot blame the older son for being jealous. The whole time they were growing up, his twerpy little brother probably got a bigger dose of Mom and Dad's attention. In recent months or years, this faithful son has had to do twice the work. As a matter of fact, do you know where he is when the homecoming party starts? He's out working in the field! Of course he's ticked! Not surprisingly, the older brother is not especially quick to forgive and forget.

Thankfully, the father doesn't blow him off. Dad knows just what to say. To paraphrase: "Son, we both know your little brother has been messing up. He deserves a good trip to the woodshed. But you have to admit, you were worried about him too. More than anything, this is a time to celebrate. By the way, I know I haven't thanked you enough for who you are and what you do. You make me proud. If you need something, just ask. What's mine is yours."

Note this effective fathering strategy. When a kid is angry and frustrated, take them aside, confirm your love, tell them how awesome they are, give them context, speak truth, and help them see the big picture.

What about you?

There will be times when your well-behaved, loving kids want to rip each other apart. Expect it. If they can work it out themselves, let them. But if not, take them one at a time to a quiet place, let them rant, and then lay out the way it is.

SEEING BOTH SIDES

"Before you criticize a man you should walk a mile in his shoes. That way, if he gets angry he will be a mile away and you'll have his shoes."

NEW TWIST ON AN OLD SAYING

The truth is that we should—in the regular course of interacting with other humans—try to see things from their perspective. Like most guys, you think your way is the right way and your opinion is the best one. Hey, you may very well be right. But if that's the vibe you throw out to the world, then you're slamming some doors that you may not want closed.

In business, you're going to spend all your time doing it the same way you always did it. Which means you're going to miss the next big thing.

In your marriage, you're going to miss out on half of the good ideas that come with having a lifelong partner. If you're not listening with an open mind, then she'll stop sharing her recommendations and opinions. That may sound like a good thing, but it most certainly is not.

In your faith journey, you will stop learning and growing. Which means when it comes time to share or defend what you believe, you will run out of ammunition early in any spiritual battle.

With your kids, you will be building walls that may never come down. When you see they're doing something in a way you wouldn't do it, don't immediately jump down their throats or proclaim failure as a father. Instead, open a dialogue about what they're doing and why.

Solomon told his son, "The first to speak in court sounds right—until the cross-examination begins" (Proverbs 18:17 NLT). That's just another way of saying, "Every issue has two sides" and "Before casting judgment on a man, walk a mile in his shoes."

What about you?

The above paragraphs are not saying, "Don't judge." They are saying, "Look at both sides of an issue before you judge." The good news is, once you have walked a mile in another man's shoes, you have earned the right to tell him that his shoes aren't comfortable, cause calluses, and are worthless for hiking the rocky trails of life. Or just maybe you'll like his shoes so much that you'll buy two pairs for yourself.

A VERY SERIOUS ASSIGNMENT

"The great man is he who does not lose his child's heart."

MENCIUS (372–289 BC)

Your assignment for today, Dad, is to do three of the following. Any three.

Skip. Skip rocks. Climb rocks. Climb a tree. Climb real high in a tree. Build a tree fort. Build a fort in your living room out of furniture, pillows, and blankets. (Use an upside-down laundry basket as a lookout tower.) Blow bubbles. Blow bubblegum bubbles. Riffle through your old baseball-card collection. Buy five new packs of baseball cards. Hold a tea party. Bake cupcakes. Eat a Twinkie. Dunk Oreos. Eat a baloney sandwich. Doodle. Chase the cat. Draw whiskers on your face. Meow at your wife. Play cat's cradle. Hula hoop. Play ring-around-the-rosy. Play hide-and-seek. Play hopscotch. Make paper airplanes. Make a cootie catcher. Make shadow puppets. Make snow angels. Build a snowman. Build a sand castle. Run through the sprinkler. Run through a pile of leaves. Run to your neighbor's house, ring their doorbell, and hide behind a bush. Leave them a plate of cookies. Play checkers.

Play 20 questions. Read a Dr. Seuss book. Give every member of your family a burbly kiss on the cheek and ask, "Do you love me?"

Oh, yeah—most important, don't do any of these things alone. Do them with one or more of your kids, age one to twenty-five.

What about you?

Remember what it was like to be a child. Consider what it really means when Jesus says, "Truly I tell you, unless you change and become like little children, you will never enter the kingdom of heaven" (Matthew 18:3).

BE DISAPPOINTED

"Then [Jesus] returned to the disciples and found them asleep. He said to Peter, 'Couldn't you watch with me even one hour?'"

MATTHEW 26:40 NLT

This is an amazing scene. Even more amazing if you consider what Jesus had already done that night. He washed feet. Broke bread. Shared wine. Confirmed his earthly mission. Pointed out the two men who would betray and deny him. Asked God if all this was really necessary. Sweat blood.

All he wanted was for a few of his chosen disciples to say awake for 60 minutes. They didn't do it. And Jesus let them know he was disappointed.

Now there's a lot more to it than that, but let's just see if there's a lesson for fathers in there someplace.

It's okay to let our kids know when they have let us down. Let me say that again, because our society suggests that we shouldn't make our kids feel bad.

It's okay to let our kids know when they have let us down.

Of course, we don't want to guilt our kids and make them feel like whale dung on a regular basis. But if we have set clear expectations and clear deadlines and have caught them in the act of dropping the ball, then we have the right—and even the responsibility—to let them know. We need to be able to say, "Mike, I asked you to do this. What's going on?" Or "Sara, this should have been done by now. I need you to make it right."

Sometimes, it's not easy being a dad. You need to figure out a way to confront your children in love, firmness, and grace.

What about you?

When there's something that really needs to be done, often a dad will just do it himself rather than risk having his son or daughter not get the job done right. That's more work for you. And less responsibility for your children. But Dad, can you see how that's a formula that steals from both you and them?

BEEN HERE, DONE THAT

"The LORD is like a father to his children,
tender and compassionate to those who fear him.
For he knows how weak we are;
he remembers we are only dust.
Our days on earth are like grass;
like wildflowers, we bloom and die.
The wind blows, and we are gone—
as though we had never been here."

PSALM 103:13-16 NLT

By my calculations there are four ways that humans can—in a way—live forever.

One, by creating something of lasting value. A significant work of art. A novel that stands the test of time. A scientific breakthrough that changes the way mankind thinks.

Two, by giving so much of yourself that your life impacts another. And their life impacts another. And their life impacts another.

Three, by having kids. And then making sure those children value family, so they also want to have kids. Etcetera.

Four, by making sure you live for eternity in heaven.

Which of the above sounds doable to you? When

the wind blows away the dust of our transient human condition, what will remain of you?

What about you?

Are you so caught up in the tyranny of the urgent that you have zero time to stop and consider your place in eternity? This life is a finger snap. Eternity is a line that goes on for...well...eternity!

MANUFACTURING GREATNESS

"There are no great men, only great challenges that ordinary men are forced by circumstances to meet."

William F. Halsey

Want your kids to do great things? Then don't let them settle for the easy way out. Schools these days seem to be more worried about minimizing fuss than challenging kids to greatness.

If little Johnny comes home with A's and B's, then his parents are not going to march down to the school and raise a fuss. So it's easier for everyone involved if the teacher doesn't put any real challenges in front of the lad. The good grades come. Everyone is happy. And an ordinary boy remains ordinary.

But if Johnny's or Janie's dad really wants them to do great things, he is going to make sure they face some challenges that are not so easy and are sometimes less than pleasant.

Examples? Cleaning the crawl space. Scrubbing the lawn chairs. Being in charge of the birdcage or litter box. Making their bed every morning. Doing their own laundry. Rewriting that English paper. Rewriting that English paper again. Joining debate, chess club, or

Model UN. Taking accelerated math or college-prep econ. Spending a season on a foreign mission field. Or finding a job outside their comfort zone.

Greatness doesn't happen by accident.

What about you?

Burdening our children with high expectations sometimes gets a bad rap. That's malarkey. If you've built a positive relationship with your kids, then you have the right and responsibility to challenge them to the next level. Kids need to know what we expect of them. Funny thing about expectations? They tend to come true.

JOIN. REJOICE. PROVIDE.

"Keep your eyes wide open before marriage, half shut afterwards."

Benjamin Franklin

We should not be so naïve to think there is only one way to build a family.

According to the 2010 U.S. Census, 69 percent of children live under one roof with both parents. Almost 23 percent live with their mother only (12 percent divorced or separated, 1 percent widowed, 10 percent never married). About 3.5 percent live with their father only. Exactly 4 percent live with neither parent.*

In every category, many of the kids are doing great. In every category, some are not. We all know parents who are getting the job done for their kids in tragic or difficult situations. Still, shouldn't we do everything possible to give our kids the best chance to succeed in life—emotionally, physically, academically, socially, and spiritually?

Statistics are readily available and are not really surprising, but here are just a few. Children of divorce are two times more likely to drop out of school or commit suicide. A child in a female-headed home is ten times

---

* www.census.gov/population/www/socdemo/hh-fam/cps2010.html.

more likely to be beaten or murdered. Teenagers in single-parent and blended families are three times more likely to need psychological help within a given year.*

So how can we possibly uncover the best plan for building a family?

> *What God has joined together, let no one separate (Mark 10:9).*
>
> *Rejoice in the wife of your youth (Proverbs 5:18).*
>
> *Children don't provide for their parents. Rather, parents provide for their children (2 Corinthians 12:14 NLT).*

Invite God to your wedding. Stay married. Find joy with your bride. Together provide for your kids. No real surprise, right?

What about you?

Did the above stats fill you with hope, determination, satisfaction...or regret? What's your next step?

---

* www.marriage-success-secrets.com/statistics-about-children-and-divorce.html.

PLUG INTO THE POWER SOURCE

"May the force be with you."

OBI-WAN KENOBI, THE *STAR WARS* MOVIES

Great movies. Bad theology. "The force" is nothing more than a gazillion-dollar empire that made George Lucas rich and famous. Beyond the special effects, it's a myth. So the question remains, where can a guy plug in for ultimate power?

Some choose the weight room or local steroid provider. Others seek power in conference rooms or stock portfolios, or by adding titles to their name. Some men sadly wield the dark side of power through physical, emotional, verbal, or sexual abuse. They all come up empty.

So how do we satisfy our power fix? Paradoxically, to gain power you need to accept your limitations. Look what happened when Paul prayed to be healed of his own most frustrating flaw.

> *He has said to me, "My grace is sufficient for you, for power is perfected in weakness." Most gladly, therefore, I will rather boast about my weaknesses, so that the power of Christ may dwell in me (2 Corinthians 12:9 NASB).*

When you realize you are weak—that you can't do anything significant by your own efforts—then you will be made strong.

What about you?

What's your power source? What are you counting on to help you get through the day? May the one true force be with you.

THOU SHALT NOT WHINE

"What have you done to us by bringing us out of Egypt? Didn't we say to you in Egypt, 'Leave us alone; let us serve the Egyptians'? It would have been better for us to serve the Egyptians than to die in the desert!"

Exodus 14:11-12

I know you're not a whiner. But I also know sometimes our thought process goes that way. "It's not fair." "Why me?" "A ticket? But I was just keeping up with traffic." "That was supposed to be *my* promotion." "Wah-wah-wah!"

In this real-life scenario from Exodus, the Israelites whining to Moses are facing death from the fast-approaching Egyptian army, so maybe we should cut them some slack. Plus, they don't know that Moses is about to lead them across the dry bottom of the Red Sea in the greatest escape in history. But they *should* know. Or at least they should trust. God always has a plan. Quite often, it's more surprising and more satisfying than anything you could ever imagine.

The book of Exodus is filled with whining and grumbling Israelites. If one of your kids is a whiner, that may be a good book to read together.

What about you?

Been whining lately? Are you saying, "Why me, God?" Look back at all he has done for you in the last decade. Sure, frustrating stuff happens. We wonder if we would be better off at our old job or even before we had kids. But his big-picture plan is solid. He truly does have your best interest in mind. And by the way, God still does miracles—large and small.

A MATTER OF TRUST

"Only he who believes is obedient.
Only he who is obedient, believes."

Dietrich Bonhoeffer

Why are we surprised when humans do nasty things to each other? The Bible tells us "all have sinned and fall short of the glory of God" (Romans 3:23). And sinners, by definition, sin. As a matter of fact, I think if I wasn't in the grip of grace I would be a really good sinner. Years ago, my brother and I used to lie in our bunk beds planning the perfect crime. Gotta admit, sin actually sounds like fun.

The only reason I strive to be obedient today is because I believe. I believe Jesus is who he says he is. And, I guess, the only reason I got to that point is because someone I trusted suggested I dig into the Bible, and I obeyed. Bonhoeffer was right.

Our kids are facing the same catch-22. They really aren't going to be obedient to you or to God unless they believe and choose to surrender to that authority. But they won't believe until they give your authority or God's authority a chance, thereby testing whether it makes sense to obey.

If you're in your own power struggle with your kids (or with God), start by understanding the link between belief and obedience. With your kids, the younger you get them to believe and obey, the easier it is!

What about you?

Too philosophical? Not really. The primary goal of any dad reading this devotional is to get his kids to believe in and obey God. If they come away trusting you, that's a bonus!

ENTERING YOUR KID'S WORLD

"In the big inning..."

GENESIS 1:1. FRACTURED

It's not a bad idea to establish yourself as a life coach for your son or daughter. Mentor. Guru. Yoda. Trail master on the road of life.

But somewhere along the line you also need to literally be a real coach. With a whistle, clipboard, and roster filled with ragtag kids who all wear the same color T-shirt once or twice a week for some kind of organized athletic endeavor.

Even if your son or daughter is a terrible athlete. Even if you're a nonathlete. Volunteer to assist. Or schedule practices. Or keep statistics. Or rake the field. (Just don't volunteer to do snacks. Real men don't organize snacks. That's what team moms are for.)

The benefits are many. You get to see your child in a new environment. You get to be close to the action, watching them grimace, grit their teeth, sweat, breathe, and stare down their opponent. You are forced to spend time with them. In the car. On the bench. Waiting out rain delays and late refs. Your young star (or nonstar) gets to see you at your best and your worst.

If your son or daughter continues on to a trophy-winning career complete with scholarships and pro contracts, you can take all the credit. You were there at the start. On the other hand, if they are just terrible and you are an even worse coach, cut your losses after one season. But have no regrets. You'll have something to laugh about together—especially when they find excellence and redemption in some nonsports arena.

Either way, hang that whistle on your tie rack and let it remind you of that championship season you spent as your kid's coach.

What about you?

If you're already doing the gung-ho coach thing, try to recruit some dads who may have not yet discovered the joy of fatherhood. Don't be pushy or preachy. Just invite them along to have some fun.

AT THE CROSSROADS

"This is what the LORD says: 'Stand at the crossroads and look; ask for the ancient paths, ask where the good way is, and walk in it, and you will find rest for your souls. But you said, "We will not walk in it."'"

JEREMIAH 6:16

See if you can detect the parallels between the people of the land of Judah and rebellious teens. It won't be difficult.

About 600 BC, Jeremiah was the top-dog prophet for the kingdom of Judah during a time the leaders and people were making some bad choices. He knew they were headed for a fall and confronted them, even condemning their actions.

In chapter after chapter, Jeremiah gives warnings and advice. He doesn't want to be the bearer of bad news, but God gives him the words to say. That clear advice includes a way to escape punishment: "Return, faithless people; I will cure you of backsliding" (Jeremiah 3:22).

In chapter 6, Jeremiah again quotes the Lord to the people. Every crossroad comes with the same question: "Are you going to take the old, sure way or choose your own path?" Choose the good way—God's way—and your soul will find rest. As it turns out, the people of Judah respond the same way a high percentage of teenagers do today: "I see your path, but I choose not to walk down it."

History confirms that Jerusalem is destroyed and Judah falls. God's chosen people are once again taken captive. This time to Babylonia. The good news for wayward teens and the people of Jerusalem is that eventually restoration does come. And when the time was right, Jesus also entered the scene.

What about you?

When your teenager faces a hazardous crossroad, it's wise to erect some warning signs and even some roadblocks. But in the end they are going to choose their own path. Be patient. But never give up on God's plan for restoration.

READY FOR THE CYNICS AND MOCKERS

"Worldly people imagine that the saints must find it difficult to live with so many restrictions, but the bondage is with the world, not with the saints."

Oswald Chambers

As your kids get older and start to own their faith, they are going to face some skeptics and naysayers. That is not a bad thing.

If your kids are only following Christ because of you, then they may be in trouble. But sooner or later (hopefully sooner) you want them to own their own faith. To know the personal advantages of living a life surrendered to Christ. Advantages for today and for eternity.

Along the way, they will have classmates and friends who don't get it. Those lost souls are very likely to repeat the same tired refrains used for centuries: "Church is for people who can't think for themselves" or "Religion is all just a bunch of rules."

Your most important job is to help your kids choose to follow Christ. Your next most important job is to help them defend their faith. From mean-spirited cynics. From true friends asking legitimate questions. And also from their own reasonable doubts that creep in as they grow in wisdom and wrestle with the great truths of life.

The Bible suggests that you—and your children—should not be intimidated by doubters and mockers. The good news is for everyone—even the naysayers. "I am not ashamed of the gospel, because it is the power of God that brings salvation to everyone who believes" (Romans 1:16).

What about you?

When the world scoffs at your beliefs, are you ready? We have a responsibility for ourselves and—until they're ready—we have a responsibility for our kids too.

HOLD TIGHT. HOLD LOOSE.

"A man can receive nothing unless it has been given him from heaven."

John the Baptist, in John 3:27 NASB

What's yours?

Got news for you. Your house, car, laptop, guitar, big-screen TV, leather jacket, credit cards, yacht, hammock, workbench, iPhone, baseball glove, and favorite coffee mug are not yours. Whether you believe in God or not, those things are on loan to you from him. So take good care of your stuff, because someday you are going to be held accountable for how it was all used.

Knowing that you really don't own any of that stuff should help you hold it loosely. Be generous. Covet not. Don't waste your life gathering more and more worldly possessions and building bigger houses to hold it all. It can all be taken from you in an instant.

Got more news for you. Your kids are also not yours.

Knowing that you really don't own your children should help you also to hold on to them loosely. And tightly. Grasp them close with everlasting hugs, endless hours of conversation, and permanent connections between your world and theirs. While simultaneously letting them go. Pray them over to God. Trust God so much that you stop forcing your plan onto your children's lives and surrender to his plan.

Heaven has given you great gifts. The best thing you can do is say "thanks" and then give them right back.

What about you?

What do you cherish? What are you holding on to most tightly? Your job title? Your hobby? Your gym membership? Your TV remote? Your sex life? Your 401K? Your status in the community or even at church? Your kids' status and accomplishments? Instead, cherish things that are eternal.

CHESTERTON'S FENCE

"Don't ever take a fence down until you know the reason it was put up."

G.K. Chesterton (1874–1936)

When's the last time you had a good old-fashioned philosophical discussion with your children? If your kids are under seven, you may want to hold off a few years. But getting your older kids to think deep thoughts is one of the great privileges of fatherhood. Tonight at dinner, can you imagine saying something like this to your kids?

"I came across this idea in a book I was reading. It's 'Chesterton's Fence.' G.K. Chesterton was a deep thinker from about 100 years ago. It was a time of great social change, and radical reformers wanted to throw out all the work done by the previous generations. They would look at an existing regulation or prohibition and discard it with little thought.

"Chesterton's response was, 'Don't ever take a fence down until you know the reason it was put up.' In other words, before you move ahead with your plan, take a step back. Look at the old plan and really seek to understand its original purpose. Then make your decision. Maybe the old fence should be taken down. But maybe not. Whaddaya think, kids?"

Of course, they may look at you like you just grew a third eye. Or they may just say, "Huh?" But the idea is to get them thinking outside themselves. At the very least, you're going to keep them guessing. And that's not a bad thing.

What about you?

Do you have dinner-table conversations *with* your kids? Or *at* your kids? Work toward the day when you can freely exchange ideas and hold friendly debates over any topic.

BEGINNING GOOD WORKS

"I thank my God every time I remember you. In all my prayers for all of you, I always pray with joy because of your partnership in the gospel from the first day until now, being confident of this, that he who began a good work in you will carry it on to completion until the day of Christ Jesus."

PHILIPPIANS 1:3-6

My kids are all out of the house. Three married. One single and working two hours away. One at West Point. They are not underfoot. They are not constantly requiring my attention. Sure, there are photos all over the house and my office, but those two-dimensional images are part of the background of life.

Still, God brings each of my kids to mind several times a day. Not constantly, but they are always near the front of my consciousness. I'm sure you're the same way. The thoughts meander. What are they doing? Are they okay? Are they having a good day? What are they celebrating? What are they worried about? Do they need my help?

This day, this hour, this season of their life, are they relying on God or pushing God away? As God brings people, resources, and fresh ideas into their lives, will they have the courage and insight to accept those gifts? Will they allow God to complete the good work he has begun in their lives?

There is no way I will ever know the answer to all those questions. With five kids, how could I? But God knows. So, that's why Paul's opening lines to the Philippians are so critical for dads. Read them again. Look at the verbs: "Remember." "Thank." "Pray." "Be confident."

Whether your kids are in preschool, grad school, or the school of life, that's a pretty good formula for dads of all ages. *Remember. Thank. Pray. Be confident.*

What about you?

Paul wrote this letter from jail to a healthy church in the city of Philippi. He couldn't stop by anyone's apartment, take them to Sunday brunch, catch a ball game, help them rewire a lamp, stroll an art fair, assemble furniture from Ikea, or play 18 holes this Saturday. With your grown kids, you can probably do any or all of these things. Some of your questions may even be answered.

SCRIPTWRITERS, TAKE NOTE

"Clear eyes. Full hearts. Can't lose."

Eric Taylor, head coach of the fictional Dillon Panthers

I miss *Friday Night Lights*. You may remember the NBC drama set in the fictional town of Dillon, Texas. It had a small but loyal following and promoted values like integrity, hard work, discipline, and fidelity. I can't do it justice here. But I can reveal that the slogan of the Dillon Panthers football team seems to be biblically based.

- *Clear eyes:* "The eye is the lamp of the body; so then if your eye is clear, your whole body will be full of light" (Matthew 6:22 NASB).
- *Full hearts:* "The eyes of the Lord range throughout the earth to strengthen those whose hearts are fully committed to him" (2 Chronicles 16:9).
- *Can't lose:* "I am convinced that neither death nor life, neither angels nor demons, neither the present nor the future, nor any powers, neither height nor depth, nor

> anything else in all creation, will be able to separate us from the love of God that is in Christ Jesus our Lord" (Romans 8:38-39).

Hey, Hollywood! Want to script some great dialogue? Try God's Word. It's inspiring, true—and you can't get sued for plagiarism.

What about you?

Where do you look for inspiration? Hollywood? Or God's holy Word?

BUSTED

"It is easier to build strong children than to repair broken men."

FREDERICK DOUGLASS

Yes, dads need to notice when our kids mess up. Sometimes we even need to take extensive corrective action. But let's not forget that kids are going to make mistakes, so let's deal with them and not dwell on them. Kids often learn from their mistakes and make changes you may not even know about. Don't assume that just because ABC once led to XYZ, every time ABC happens XYZ will follow.

Your best course of action is probably to tell the deep recesses of your brain to be on constant alert for any signs of ABC or XYZ in your kids as well as their friends. But—and this is the hard part—keep those thoughts and concerns away from the front of your brain. In your day-to-day life, assume that XYZ will never happen again.

If you're thoroughly confused, let me weave a fictional tale. Your wonderful 17-year-old son, Jethro, makes a pretty good buck fixing bikes at the bike store. It's not a secret that he has $600 in the book under his nightstand. On the same night he sleeps over at Horatio's house, you discover the book now has about half that amount. Jethro never was a good liar. Plus...your spies informed you that kids have been buying fake IDs. Plus...you could tell he had been drinking because you're a good parent and you know your kid. Jethro is busted. Punishment is paid. Horatio is out of the picture. Jethro admits his mistake and is genuinely sorry.

Well done. That's how families work. You didn't overreact. A lesson was learned. Trust is reestablished.

Now, here's the point. When more money is missing, or Horatio's name comes up, or Jethro sleeps late on a Saturday, don't assume the worst. Maybe there's a reasonable explanation. Maybe this is really a God-given chance to demonstrate to your sincerely repentant son that your relationship is returning to its former strength.

Don't accuse. Don't interrogate. Don't panic.

But do check with your spies.

What about you?

One of the reasons God gave families two parents is so that the two of you can strategize, circle the wagons, react without losing your cool, have long talks with your teenager, agree on and enforce punishments, and come out healthier on the other side.

SILENT PICTURES

"Silence is the most perfect expression of scorn."

George Bernard Shaw

There was a time when fathers who were the "strong, silent type" were held in the highest esteem. Their silence was perceived as a sign of strength. Whether they came home from work in overalls, a gray flannel suit, or a military uniform, they were not greeted at the door with a cacophony of hugs and laughter. As a matter of fact, when Papa came home the kids might be already tucked in bed or be told to "let your father rest—he's worked hard all day."

These men fathered from a distance, or not at all. Moms did the day-to-day child rearing. These silent fathers were called upon only when a dose of discipline was needed. Fear was the motivator. Relationship was out of the question.

I'm guessing you are not that kind of dad. Still, what's your takeaway from such an image? Was that your father? Are you glad those days are over? Or do you wish your children did approach you with a little more awe and reverence? On some days, do you think you're not getting the respect you deserve?

Let's strike a balance, men. The goal is relationship and respect.

How do you get both? Availability, acceptance, and love lead to relationship. Consistency, protection, and accountability lead to respect.

Lots of big words there, Dad. But park on each one for a moment and consider where you may or may not be getting the job done.

What about you?

If your dad was the strong, silent type, you may be tempted to lament a lack of hugs and laughter in your boyhood home. Instead, I recommend you cut him some slack. As long as he wasn't hostile or oppressive, be grateful for the provision, protection, and strength of character he brought to the family.

CALLING ALL TREASURE HUNTERS

"I've got all the money I'll ever need, just so long as I die by four o'clock."

Henny Youngman

The Bible has some 500 verses concerning faith and about 500 on the topic of prayer. But more than 2300 on money and possessions. Here are just a few:

> *Whoever loves money never has money enough; whoever loves wealth is never satisfied with his income (Ecclesiastes 5:10).*
>
> *No one can serve two masters. Either he will hate the one and love the other, or he will be devoted to the one and despise the other. You cannot serve both God and Money (Matthew 6:24).*
>
> *The love of money is a root of all kinds of evil. Some people, eager for money, have wandered from the faith and pierced themselves with many griefs (1 Timothy 6:10).*
>
> *Where your treasure is, there your heart will be also (Luke 12:34).*

What do you love? Who is your master? Where is

your treasure? In our culture, money has a stranglehold on most guys. To break that grip, we need to recognize the temporal nature of possessions. Earthly stuff doesn't last. What does? God. Our souls. Relationships. Love.

What about you?

When you envision success for your children, do you envision a well-paying job with a big house? Or do you visualize your grown kids with a strong faith and humble, grateful hearts?

A BETTER USE FOR CELL PHONES

"A father is a guy who has snapshots in his wallet where his money used to be."

UNKNOWN

This great quote was obviously coined before smartphones and iPods. A few years back, it was a significant challenge for dads to carry current, nonembarrassing photos of their offspring. Sure, most kids had school photos taken every year, but they were usually pretty goofy-looking. Plus, they never seemed to fit in those translucent photo holders that used to come with most new wallets.

Based on my informal surveys taken when my kids were young, most dads—including me—didn't do well keeping up-to-date pix of the kids in our billfolds. It was something we always intended to do, but the hassle got in the way.

With the advent of digital phone technology, today's dad has no excuse.

I'm quite certain you carry a device that allows you to store and even capture current photos of those growing kids you love so much. So make sure you're doing exactly that. Make sure you've got some serious and some silly snapshots of your babies, toddlers, rug rats, tweens, teens, and beyond. Start by downloading an ultrasound screen shot of your baby in utero and never stop.

Your pocketful of digital photos will then always be available to whip out and show to other dads when they start bragging about their kids. After all, your kids are smarter and better-looking. But more important than that are the times when you flip through a file of photos just for your own amusement.

Between phone calls, at stoplights, on elevators, sitting at the fast-food lunch counter, or in the dark of your hotel room when you're away from home. As you smile considering each of those treasured faces, take a moment to lift each of them up in prayer. And then ask God to also make you the kind of dad they need.

What about you?

Even if your kids don't like having their picture taken, they do like the idea that Dad has family photos in his smartphone. If you ever see me at an airport or conference, ask to see my kids. I'll show you mine if you show me yours.

A FEW REASONABLE WORDS

"One ought, every day at least, to hear a little song, read a good poem, see a fine picture, and if it were possible, to speak a few reasonable words."

JOHANN WOLFGANG VON GOETHE (1749–1832)

I would add to the above, "Dad, do all those things with a child."

One of the great joys of being dads is watching our children discover new things. We make a great fuss over their first steps and their first day of school and rightfully so. But often it's the small day-to-day moments that add up to the most satisfying memories. Hearing a clever rhyme. Swaying to a catchy tune. Noting how one swirl of a paintbrush can draw your eye across canvas. Taking the time to articulate a new thought. Pondering an emerging doubt or healthy skepticism. Discovering the melodic flow of words that form a satisfying poetic meter.

Goethe (approximate pronunciation, *GER-tuh*) was right. He has pointed out a reasonable list of simple yet profound events that ought to be done every day. These things will not happen without some level of intentionality. If we hit the pillow at night and grunt *same-old same-old*, we've lost that day.

If you have a small child at home—or even a teenager—be intentional about entering their world once a day and sharing a song, a phrase, an image, or thought. They will be better for it. And so will you.

What about you?

It's a matter of persistent parenting. Starting today, be intentional about sharing something you've discovered with your little one. Before long, they will be discovering things they want to share with you.

LAUGHTER IS THE BEST WEAPON

"Humor is a rubber sword—it allows you to make a point without drawing blood."

MARY HIRSCH

Careful here, Dad. Sarcasm ain't funny. Making fun of your daughter's new hairstyle is not a good idea. Joking with your son about his falling batting average is a formula for a cold shoulder.

On the other hand, a little laughter will often help defuse an uncomfortable situation. When your two middle-schoolers are arguing about what TV program to watch, you could insist on watching the Shirley Temple movie marathon. When your 17-year-old daughter whines that her car (which you bought for her) isn't swanky enough, reminisce how you walked ten miles to school in the snow, uphill both ways. When your 7-year-old won't eat his asparagus, grab a stalk from your plate and challenge him to a fencing duel. Loser must finish his veggies.

Humor works. But don't make your kid the punch line. The best humor for dads is the self-deprecating kind in which the laughter is directed back at you.

Dad, I think you can take it. Especially if your kids are laughing right along with you.

What about you?

If you find yourself mocking or teasing your kid, back off. It may be impossible to know when they're okay with it. Or when their spirit or self-image is being crushed. Better to make yourself the butt of jokes. And just laugh it off.

SOMETHING TO FIGHT FOR

"While women weep, as they do now, I'll fight. While little children go hungry, as they do now, I'll fight. While men go to prison, in and out, in and out, as they do now, I'll fight. While there is a drunkard left, while there is a poor lost girl upon the streets, while there remains one dark soul without the light of God, I'll fight. I'll fight to the very end!"

WILLIAM BOOTH

The words above are from the last public address by William Booth, founder of the Salvation Army. By his death in 1912, that organization was at work in 58 countries. Today, more than 3.4 million volunteers led by 3500 officers assist more than 29 million people in need each year. Their services include disaster relief, shelters for battered women, day camps, family counseling, prison ministry, substance-abuse rehabilitation, and sharing the gospel in 160 languages.

What's most interesting about Booth's words is the source. You may recognize them as inspired by the Gospel of Matthew:

I was hungry, and you fed me. I was thirsty, and you gave me a drink. I was a stranger, and you invited me into your home. I was naked, and you gave me clothing. I was sick, and you cared for me. I was in prison, and you visited me (Matthew 25:35-36 NLT).

Booth took Jesus' words, saw their relevance in today's world, and then turned them into a personal pledge complete with a promise of action.

That's a pretty good way to study Scripture. Assume the words you read are meant for today. Make them personal. Turn them into fighting words. Stick with it until your last day on earth.

Suddenly that family Bible study you've been meaning to launch has a purpose beyond deep spiritual thoughts. It may lead you and your family to even deeper Spirit-led actions.

What about you?

Oh yeah, if you're really inspired, go to SalvationArmyUSA.org and consider volunteer opportunities.

A FURNACE OF DOUBT

"It is not as a child that I believe and confess Jesus Christ. My hosanna is born of a furnace of doubt."

FYODOR DOSTOYEVSKY

The famed nineteenth-century Russian writer Dostoyevsky explored some deep themes in his writings. The definition of freedom. The existence of God. The responsibility of the individual. An ongoing conflict between body and spirit.

Worth noting is that Fyodor's father was a doctor and devout Christian. But that didn't make Fyodor a Christian (or a doctor for that matter). He had to work such things out for himself.

Like a lot of twentysomethings throughout history, Dostoyevsky started thinking "deep thoughts" while hanging out with progressive intellectual poets and radicals eager to introduce socialism and even revolution. Those meetings earned him exile to Siberia and even a mock execution, in which he was forced to face his own mortality.

During his five years in that labor camp, the writer-philosopher stopped trying to explain God and surrendered to God, describing his conversion experience in later writings. When he died a quarter century later, the

New Testament he'd acquired in Siberia was on his lap and John 12:24 was carved on his tombstone:

> *Truly, truly, I say to you, unless a grain of wheat falls into the earth and dies, it remains alone; but if it dies, it bears much fruit (John 12:24 NASB)*

Dad, young people have always had to find their own way. Sometimes it even takes five years of hard labor in a frozen wasteland or facing a mock firing squad. If you can rescue your kids from such things, please do. But don't rescue them so much that they never realize their need for God.

What about you?

Under what dire circumstance did you finally realize your need for a Savior? Your story may not be as dramatic as Fyodor Dostoyevsky's, but it may be worth sharing with your family.

THE SILENT TREATMENT

"The LORD *will fight for you;*
you need only to be still."

EXODUS 14:14

This great quote is from Moses' address to the Israelites on the edge of the Red Sea. The two million men, women, and children had only recently escaped from Egypt and were terrified as they watched the entire Egyptian army marching in their direction. They had no plan. They had no time. And they had no way out. But they did have a leader with confidence.

For the record, Moses also did not have a plan. But he did have something that the rest of Israelites apparently lacked. Faith in God. He had seen God's intervention in his own life and in the life of the Israelites. But not only had he witnessed the work of God…he remembered it.

Moments later, God told Moses to raise his staff and stretch his hand over the sea to divide the water. You know the rest of the story.

Yes, Moses had to listen and obey. Yes, the Israelites had to move through the dry seabed under their own power. Yes, they still had all kinds of unanswered questions. But they were also part of one of the greatest escapes in the history of the world.

So if you find yourself between a rock and a hard place—or between the Red Sea and the Egyptian army—your best option is to just say a silent prayer, keep your mouth shut, and do what God tells you to do.

What about you?

Caught between work and home? Between utility bills and a much-needed vacation? Between your local school district and your faith? Consider stopping for a moment and allowing the Lord to lay out your next step.

BE THERE FOR THE PROCESS

"Failure is simply the opportunity to begin again, this time more intelligently."

HENRY FORD

How to respond when one of your kids fails is one of the great challenges of fatherhood. You want them to get back on the horse. You want them to tough it out and try and try again. But you also know that sometimes the right thing to do is take a step back and not push too hard. Maybe your daughter isn't going to be the next Mary Lou Retton. Maybe your son isn't going to be a state champion wrestler.

Dad, the only way you'll know is if you've invested in the day-to-day routine. If you just show up at the final match or end-of-season competition, then you have no idea what to expect. You may swagger in with the anticipation of victory, but that may be unrealistic. When they come up short—or even if they win—you feel out of the loop and ill-equipped to deliver the right kind of comfort or congratulations.

Want to really enjoy your child's victories? Or offer the right kind of support when they lose? Then be there for *the process*. Once in a while, stick around and watch their practices. Talk about their goals in the car ride home. Volunteer to be an assistant coach. Watch videos and read how-to books. Help them with a drill or invest in some professional-quality gear. Don't push. Partner.

What about you?

It's easy to cheer a winner from the sidelines. The tough part is seeing victory even in defeat. Once again, it's a matter of putting in the time and earning the right to give advice and offer condolences.

NURTURING DREAM-CHASERS

"Orville Wright didn't have a pilot's license."

Richard Tait

Most dads understand the value of warning labels, multipage instructions, and posted restrictions. You recognize that warnings have value. They help make sure fewer kids fall out of roller coasters, salmonella won't spoil your picnic, and pizzas are golden brown on the bottom and properly melted and gooey on top.

Your kids, on the other hand, have a distrust for authority and rules. They want to explore new vistas and soar to new heights. They don't want to hear that it's a bad idea to make toaster waffles in the bathtub or jump off the garage roof with a bedsheet parachute.

Our kids see just about every authority figure as a force that stifles creativity and ingenuity.

Dad, as your kids chase their dreams, it's up to you to be more of an encourager than naysayer. Early on, set yourself up as a voice they want to listen to. Point out opportunities and possibilities. Invest yourself emotionally—and maybe financially—in their earliest endeavors. Earn their trust early, and when the time is right you'll be able to point out possible pitfalls and provide warnings that need to be given.

Consider the great inventors, pioneers, and entrepreneurs of history. I suppose it's possible that their motivation and drive came from trying to prove their old man wrong. But I like to think that most of them would say, "I owe it all to my father, who encouraged me to chase my dreams."

What about you?

Imagine your kid coming to you with a slightly crazy idea. Is your first impulse to throw up warnings and roadblocks? Or would you listen, nod your head, and say, "Wow. That's fantastic. Let me know if I can help in any way!"

THE VIEW FROM ABOVE

"'My thoughts are not your thoughts, neither are your ways my ways,' declares the LORD. 'As the heavens are higher than the earth, so are my ways higher than your ways, and my thoughts than your thoughts.'"

ISAIAH 55:8-9

This may be one of those lessons better told by a mom, but it's so revealing that it's worth including here.

Imagine a young lad sitting at the foot of his momma's rocking chair. The fireplace is crackling, and she's relaxing with some embroidery after a long day. The boy looks up quizzically as his momma's hand moves the needle in and through the delicate tapestry. What does he see? From below, her handiwork looks like a formless, purposeless, and tangled zigzag of knots and loose threads. But when the boy says, "Whatcha doin', Momma?" his momma smiles and tilts the embroidery hoop up to reveal a charming garden scene outlined by a few well-chosen words of wisdom.

The view from below is confusing; the view from above makes perfect sense.

Just so it is when we compare our perspective with God's. Much of our messy lives are filled with loose threads, zigzags, and knots. Times when we have lost our way, changed our minds, and stopped in our tracks. But a heavenly perspective—one we cannot possibly have yet—reveals perfect order.

At the end of our lives, we'll see how God's handiwork comes together in complete perfection. Until then, we'll have to trust the Creator to keep crafting the story of our lives. Occasionally we'll get a glimpse of his entire plan for our lives, but only if we rest at his feet, lift our eyes with trust and expectation, and say, "Whatcha doin', Papa?"

What about you?

It's a great word picture. And it's a visual image you should definitely share with your kids. But when? Maybe today. Maybe when they ask why bad things happen to good people. Maybe when you pass a wall of framed cross-stitch at the county-fair craft booths. One thing is sure, you'll never share it unless you spend time living life with your kids.

KIDS THESE DAYS

"If it feels good, do it."

SLOGAN OF THE 1960S

Looking at it now, there's a happy-go-lucky vibe to that 50-year-old concept. It's almost cute in its innocence.

Today's young adults have developed a similar mantra, but it's delivered in a darker, in-your-face tone. It goes something like this: "Who's to say what's right or wrong? Don't you dare impose your values on me."

Twentysomethings in our world have been taught to believe that church, prayer, God, and absolute truth are okay for some people. But most of them don't see the point.

Today's teenagers have taken a step even deeper into the abyss. The twenty-first-century culture says, "Religion is for fools." Worse, that notion is delivered in a derisive, mocking tone with no hesitation or fear.

Our younger kids may grow up in a world that pays no heed to religion. It's a nonissue. They may not even waste any breath on the debate.

Don't panic quite yet. All is not lost. But clearly we can't just pretend that our children are going to see the crucial nature of a life with God without reaching some kind of turning point.

It might be when they hit bottom, forced to cry out

for a savior. Of course, no parent wants to wish that on their children.

The preferred option is that they see how having God, God's laws, God's people, and God's plan in their lives makes life better. If that sounds too obvious, maybe that's because it is. Once you receive Christ into your life, there's a refreshing clarity that allows you to look at where you were and where you are.

In other words, knowing Christ feels good. And you know what they say: "If it feels good, do it."

What about you?

Sometimes we make religion too hard. Perhaps we should present God's grace as easy.

FINANCIAL ACUMEN 101

"Fools spend whatever they get."

PROVERBS 21:20 NLT

This verse reminds me of an old parenting trick that delivers a practical lesson on money. It comes from Jonathan Clements, wealth-management consultant and former columnist for the *Wall Street Journal*. And the best part is, you don't have to lecture. They learn the principle all by themselves.

The basic idea is to "make your kids feel like they're spending their own money." When your nine-year-old goes on a class field trip, you expect them to ask you for lunch and spending money. Dutifully, you peel a ten or twenty out of your money clip.

But here's where the life lesson takes a valuable detour. Don't just give it to them and say, "Have a good time." They'll gladly spend your hard-earned cash, and you will have reinforced the perception that money grows on trees. Also don't say, "Bring me back the change." They'll keep spending that day until it's gone, and you'll be lucky to get back 37 cents.

Instead, look them in the eye and say, "This is now your money. It's my gift to you. Whatever you don't spend on the field trip is yours for something you may need or want later. Have a great time. I want to hear all about it when you get home." At the cafeteria your sharp child will dine sensibly. When they get to the museum gift shop, they'll think twice before buying the dust-collecting plastic dinosaur or genuine artificial Native American tomahawk made in China.

If they save a few bucks that's great. If they blow it all that day, there's a good chance they'll have a twinge of regret and come away with a real-life lesson.

And Dad, don't forget to ask them all about their adventurous day.

What about you?

Dad, you are the right man for the job when it comes to teaching your kids about money, wealth, savings, God's provision, and tithing. Remember that money is not the root of all evil. It's "the love of money that is the root of all kinds of evil" (1 Timothy 6:10 NLT)

LOCK THE DOOR. DOUSE THE LIGHTS.

"Be kind to your mother-in-law, and if necessary pay for her board at some good hotel."

Josh Billings (1818–1885)

There's a kernel of truth in all those mother-in-law jokes. Your bride's mother has opinions and suggestions on how you and her daughter should be raising your family. She may keep those ideas to herself or share them abrasively. Her ideas might be wise and wonderful. Or she may be clueless.

In any case, you need to have a plan when your efforts to build a healthy, independent family are threatened because your bride's mom insists on sticking her nose into your family business. However…

News flash: Your family is not independent.

News flash #2: Your family *is* your mother-in-law's business.

Extended families should expect to be interdependent. You should actually want your mom-in-law to sweep into your lives on occasion with gifts, baked goods, photos, housekeeping hints, child-raising expertise, and stories from when your bride was a little girl.

Yes, but. What if there is evil intent? What if the old

bag is doing damage to the health and sanity of your family? As you do in all things, you and your bride need to unite, pool your wisdom and experience, and together decide how to handle this threat to your well-being.

But probably she's not that bad. So unlock the door. Force a smile. Look for the good. And let your wife take most of the lead in how to handle her mom.

What about you?

In Matthew 8:14-15, Jesus healed Peter's mother-in-law, so there must be something worth salvaging about your bride's mum.

WHO GETS THE GLORY? WHO GETS THE BLAME?

"Let your light shine before men in such a way that they may see your good works, and glorify your Father who is in heaven."

MATTHEW 5:16 NASB

Jesus starts the famed "Sermon on the Mount" with the Beatitudes. At first reading, they are a little confusing. The meek inheriting the earth. To see God, you need a pure heart—whatever that is. And people who are blessed all seem to have some kind of need. They're hungry, thirsty, mourning, or persecuted.

A couple verses later we find more metaphorical images. We're supposed to be salt and light to the world. Salt is a preservative and brings out flavor. That sort of makes sense. Light, of course, helps people know the way.

Then comes verse 16. A sentence that just might be a formula for life, our reason for being on the planet. We are supposed to let our light shine. We are called to live and act in a way that people look at us and say, "He's a good man." But we can't stop there. We need to identify ourselves as Christians so that God gets the credit for our good works.

If we do good works without acknowledging who

we serve, than we get the glory ourselves. That's not a good plan.

So maybe we should be more outspoken about identifying ourselves as Christians. Maybe we should take ethical stands at work. Maybe we should be known as the guy who reads his Bible at lunch and doesn't go to casinos, bars, and strip clubs. Maybe we should have a fish on our car.

Of course, you know the problem. As soon as you identify yourself as a Christian, the stakes go way up. Your good works will glorify God. Your not-so-good works may give others one more reason to say, "Christians are all hypocrites." Yikes.

What about you?

What face are you putting out there to the world? Maybe you should be hiding your Christian identity. A better question: What face are you putting out there to your kids? That identity you cannot hide. Double yikes.

DAD RULES

"If someone has a stubborn and rebellious son... all the men of his town are to stone him to death."

DEUTERONOMY 21:18,21

This is a fun little diagnostic quiz for dads. Consider the two-word phrase "Dad Rules." Say it aloud. What does it mean? Where did you place the emphasis?

There are actually three interpretations of that phrase. The one you choose may—or may not—say a lot about you.

Dad #1 slaps an exclamation point onto the end and says, "Dad RULES!" Gotta like this guy. He loves life. He parties, but it's all in good fun. He knows the power of fatherhood. He is a great dad unless...unless he rules with an iron fist that comes down hard and often. If he is yelling, "Dad RULES!" with a grimace, then kids beware.

Dad #2 sees the two words and immediately thinks of a list of obligations for fathers. Rules for dad. Things like *bring home a paycheck, mow the lawn, sit in the stands and cheer, keep the vehicles maintained, buy your wife candy and flowers on Valentine's Day,* and so on. I don't know if I want to be this guy. Shouldn't fathering be more creative and spur-of-the-moment?

Dad #3 also sees those two words as a list of

obligations: rules from a dad for his kids. Under that kind of dad rules you'll find *Turn lights off when you leave the room. Don't leave the gas tank on empty. Elbows off the table. If you borrow my tools, you darn well better put them back.* This guy is okay to live with as long as he pronounces his rules with a smile on his face.

So how did you score? In the end, you probably want to carry a little of all three of those dads in your fathering toolbox. Just make sure to leave this guy out of it: "Dad Rules?"

What about you?

Actually, "Dad Rules" was the working title of my first book for fathers. Harvest House said they would publish it if we changed the name. A year later, that manuscript became the bestselling *52 Things Kids Need from a Dad*. I think you'll agree that title is a little less confusing than "Dad Rules."

NEW BEGINNINGS

"Being a Christian is more than just an instantaneous conversion—it is a daily process whereby you grow to be more and more like Christ."

Billy Graham

When one of your children comes to faith in Christ, celebrate. Let them know you are looking forward to seeing how God uses them. Encourage them to ask any and all questions. Over the course of a week or so, read the Gospel of John aloud with them. Explain to them how the Holy Spirit is now a guiding resource for their life. Open your Bible to Galatians 5:16-25 and read how life in the Spirit replaces our sinful nature with the fruit of the Spirit: love, joy, peace, patience, kindness, goodness, faithfulness, gentleness, and self-control.

At the right time, acknowledge that their life is not going to suddenly be perfect. It may even be more difficult. Keep this verse close, ready to share with prudence and discretion: "You do not belong to the world, but I have chosen you out of the world. That is why the world hates you" (John 15:19).

Do let them know that their new life in Christ may bring brand-new feelings and emotions. Or it might not. Some young people may want to share their new faith right away. For others, the Holy Spirit may be telling them to spend time getting used to their new life in Christ.

The important thing is for all new believers to make full use of the resources and experiences God makes available. Daily prayer. Regular Bible study. Worship among a local body of Christ. Tell others about the things God is doing in their life. Seek wisdom and guidance from mature believers. Trust that God will never leave them nor forsake them (Hebrews 13:5).

What about you?

If and when you have a child who trusts Jesus, write them a letter. Maybe include some of the thoughts above, adding your own words of love, joy, anticipation, and pride.

LIVING FOR THREE-DAY WEEKENDS

"Whatever you do, work at it with all your heart, as working for the Lord, not for human masters, since you know that you will receive an inheritance from the Lord as a reward. It is the Lord Christ you are serving."

COLOSSIANS 3:23-24

Are you a T.G.I.F. guy? Do you pretty much hate your job and live for weekends (which means you live five-sevenths of your life in a state of suspended animation)?

What does that say to your kids? Do you really want them to think it's okay to have a job that drags you down and gives you nothing but a paycheck? Of course, there are aspects of all jobs and careers that are not fun. But that's not what we're talking about. Men, your job is an extension of who you are, and your kids are watching and learning. Even if you hate your job for the time being, don't drag that misery home with you.

Two points to make: First, do everything possible to match your giftedness, passions, and abilities with your chosen career. Clearly that increases your chances for job satisfaction (and success, by the way.) Second, do your work "with all your heart, as working for the Lord." Serve your boss and your clients as a service to God. You could even make work an act of worship.

Finally, about those three-day weekends you love so much. Forget about living for Mondays off because of President's Day, Memorial Day, or Labor Day. The three-day weekend you should be anticipating and excited about is the one described in 1 Corinthians: "Christ died for our sins, just as the Scriptures said. He was buried, and he was raised from the dead on the third day" (1 Corinthians 15:3-4 NLT). That's a three-day weekend worth living for.

What about you?

Bosses and co-workers got you down? Welcome to the human race. (Or the rat race.) A heavenly perspective and kids waiting to hug you at the door can make all the difference.

WANNA HAVE A CATCH?

"If you build it, he will come."

The whisper in Ray Kinsella's cornfield

The fathering deficit is well documented.

One-third of America's 72 million children will go to bed without their biological father in the home. Eighty-five percent of all youths in prison and 75 percent of all adolescent patients in chemical-abuse centers grew up without a dad at home. Adolescent females 15 to 19 years old who are raised in homes without fathers are significantly more likely to engage in premarital sex.*

Way too many boys and girls are growing up without their father. Not your kids, right? Right?

Gentlemen, I hope you don't have to be reminded that having the same address as your kids does not mean you're fulfilling your obligation as a father. There's a difference between your presence and your involvement. Making rules is not the same as building a relationship. Don't confuse lecturing with conversation. If you're reading the newspaper, hiding in your workshop,

* 1996 U.S. Census report; Fulton County, Georgia, jail populations, Texas Dept. of Corrections, 1992; Rainbows for All God's Children; John O.G. Billy, Karin L. Brewster, and William R. Grady, "Contextual Effects on the Sexual Behavior of Adolescent Women," *Journal of Marriage and Family* 56 (1994).

zoned out on your fifth football game of the weekend, napping on the couch, hunkered down over a laptop, or sprawled under the hood of your nearly-rebuilt '72 Camaro, then you are not really home.

In the 1989 classic movie *Field of Dreams*, Kevin Costner's character, Ray Kinsella, did have a father growing up, but the old ballplayer just pushed his teenage son too hard. Driving a VW van back from Boston, Ray tells author Terence Mann, played by James Earl Jones, that he left home at 17 and never saw his dad again. Decades later, Ray plows under his cornfield, just to have a game of catch and make a connection with his father one more time.

Dad, I encourage you to do whatever it takes to stay connected to your kids.

What about you?

Don't make your children plow under their corn. Don't make them come looking for you. Don't make them live a life of regret. And, oh yeah, is there something you should do this year to connect or reconnect with *your* old man?

GET YOURSELF ANOTHER COUNSELOR

"This above all: to thine own self be true."

POLONIUS'S ADVICE TO HIS SON, LAERTES
HAMLET, *ACT 1, SCENE 3, WILLIAM SHAKESPEARE*

Surprise. This quote is not from the Bible. As a matter of fact, it's just about the opposite of anything Scripture says. Where you will hear this kind of advice is in teen magazines, on Facebook comments, and from school counselors who are no longer allowed to take a moral stand but still try to guide young people through the tough decisions of life. The pop phrase today is "Be true to yourself. You have to do what you think is right." Yikes. The last thing I want most teenagers to do is what they "think is right." In many cases, I'm hoping some teens do the opposite of what their gut tells them to do.

Actually, the same is true for most people. Even dads. You have to agree that, usually, when left to our own best instincts, we stink.

Not surprisingly, a better plan can be found in God's Word:

> *Do nothing out of selfish ambition or vain conceit. Rather, in humility value others above yourselves, not looking to your own interests but each of you*

to the interests of the others. In your relationships with one another, have the same mindset as Christ Jesus: Who, being in very nature God, did not consider equality with God something to be used to his own advantage; rather, he made himself nothing by taking the very nature of a servant, being made in human likeness. And being found in appearance as a man, he humbled himself by becoming obedient to death—even death on a cross! (Philippians 2:3-8).

Of course, if you're an authentic believer then maybe you *should* do what your gut tells you. But really that's not you doing the thinking, that's the guidance of the Holy Spirit, whom you received when you accepted Christ as your Savior.

What about you?

In John 14:16-17, Jesus promises to ask the Father to "give you another advocate to help you and be with you forever—the Spirit of truth." So, Dad—got Spirit?

DON'T LOOK BACK

"Seek first his kingdom and his righteousness, and all these things will be given to you as well."

MATTHEW 6:33

There's a great story in Luke, chapter 9, about a dude who actually had the audacity to tell Jesus to wait. Jesus himself is drafting disciples. One recruit says, "Yes, Lord, I will follow you, but first let me say goodbye to my family."

Jesus' reply doesn't pull any punches. He says, "Anyone who puts a hand to the plow and then looks back is not fit for the Kingdom of God" (Luke 9:61-62 NLT).

Does that sound a little mean? No. It's just honest. Once you decide to follow Jesus, keep your eyes on him. Put Christ ahead of everything—even your family. And frankly, there's no reason to look back. God is in control. He is going to take care of the situation. If your family is supposed to be part of your ministry, there's no reason to say goodbye. They'll be working alongside you before you know it. If your family would be a distraction to God's call on your life, then you must be willing to abandon everything.

Seek first God's kingdom, and he will provide everything you need. Including peace about your family.

What about you?

Might some of us really be called to abandon our family? I'm pretty sure the young man in the story is a single guy who is being called away from his father, mother, and siblings. So yes, young people being called away from their family is a typical missional calling. I'm fairly confident that Jesus would not be calling a husband to abandon his wife and kids. A husband and wife become one flesh (Genesis 2:24). Children are a gift from the Lord (Psalm 127:3). So Dad, lead your family and seek God's kingdom...together!

SCARING EXPECTANT DADS

"A baby is God's opinion that life should go on."

CARL SANDBURG

Needy wife. Slightly bewildered soon-to-be dad. False labor. Nesting. Useless breathing techniques. Angry transition. Possible Caesarean. Mind-blowing delivery. APGAR score. Counting fingers and toes. Phone call to grandparents. Eye contact. Short hospital stay. Car seat. Postpartum. Two a.m. feedings. Colic. Swaddling. Bouncy chairs. Sleeping through the night! Changing tables. Spitting up. Running out of diapers. Rolling over. Plugging outlets. Crawling. Rolling a ball. Crawling fast. Pots and pans. First word is not "dad." Standing. Teetering. Walking. Grabbing stuff. Warm, red cheeks. Not-so-terrible twos. Wagons. Mimicking. Running. Board books. Sentences. Tricycles. Singing. Scribbling. Lots of hugs and kisses. Bedtime stories. Dancing. Cousins. Friends. Drawing pictures of the family. Play dates. Keyboards. Nursery school. New friends. Imaginary friends. Jesus loves me, this I know. Birthday parties. Holidays. Soccer. Flashcards. Candy Land. Colors. ABCs. Kindergarten. Pledge of Allegiance. Phonics. Catching a ball. Throwing up.

Reading their name. Drawing hearts. Dr. Seuss. Swimming. Addition. Geography. Bible verses. Computers. Plastic baseball bats. Opinions on clothes. Mud. Strangers. Questions about God. Subtraction. Homework. Report cards. Friends moving away. Spelling. Goldfish, gerbil, guinea pig, dog, cat. Best friends. Hurt feelings. Multiplication tables. Long division. Baking. Tryouts. Piano lessons. Astronomy. Two-wheel bike. Questions about Jesus. Abstract thinking. Justice. Freedom. Worldview. Middle school. High school. Driving. Dating. College. Military. Work. Weddings. Phone call from the new dad.

What about you?

Two things to remember: Every stage is better than the last. Every year goes faster than the one before.

GOOD NEWS ABOUT THE GOOD NEWS

"You will receive power when the Holy Spirit comes on you; and you will be my witnesses in Jerusalem, and in all Judea and Samaria, and to the ends of the earth."

ACTS 1:8

Remember those awkward or challenging moments in the days right after you asked Christ to be your Lord and Savior? If you were eight or nine, maybe you went along with the flow and it felt like part of the natural progression of life. Still exciting, but your new Christian walk really didn't change the patterns of daily existence. But if you were older, you may have experienced some jolts, stumbling blocks, or moments of confusion or even regret.

Some new Christians become a little too aggressive with the gospel message. They want to share their joy with the world. Some are a little embarrassed and tell only their closest friends. Some are tongue-tied the first time they pray out loud in a small group. For sure, almost all new believers misquote Scripture or take some Bible verse completely out of context. Like many Christians, including me, you may have stories of losing your first debate about the infallibility of the Bible with some pseudo-intellectual atheist you met on a plane or faced in a dorm-room discussion. Defending your faith can be intimidating.

The good news is that God can still use you and everything you say. We're called—and equipped—to be his witnesses all the way to the ends of the earth. The Bible teaches us,

> *Do not worry about how or what you are to say; for it will be given to you in that hour what you are to say. For it is not you who speak, but it is the Spirit of your Father who speaks in you (Matthew 10:19-20 NASB).*

What about you?

If you wait until you're ready to have kids, you'll never have kids. There are just too many unknowns. Similarly, if you wait until you're 100 percent ready to talk about your faith with others, you will never be ready. Yes, prepare. Yes, study and spend time with mature believers. But don't be anxious. You have the Holy Spirit on your side.

LIGHT TO YOUR CAREER PATH

"Every child is an artist. The problem is how to remain an artist once he grows up."

Pablo Picasso

Are you the kind of dad who might push your kids toward more practical careers like business, engineering, nursing, accounting, and so on?

Well, what if your son or daughter is an artist at heart? Or has a legitimate chance to make it as an athlete, musician, or actor? What if God is clearly calling them to pursue a soul-satisfying career that is completely outside your own area of expertise? Forest ranger. Bricklayer. Archaeologist. Audio engineer.

One of the toughest things a dad must do is open doors to careers that he just doesn't understand. Take a poll of a dozen adult friends. You will be surprised how many of them began a course of study—or remain in a career—just because they thought they had no choice. They'll say, "It's something my father wanted me to do."

Of course, they may be good at their job. It may be the exact right thing for them. But still they wonder. They have some leftover what-ifs that may never go away. (Perhaps we all have some of those.)

At this point, we could consider a verse we explored earlier, Proverbs 22:6, which challenges parents to "train up a child in the way he should go" (NASB).

But perhaps even more important is this idea from the book of Titus. Whatever career path they choose, we need to challenge them

> *to be an example of good deeds, with purity in doctrine, dignified, sound in speech which is beyond reproach...to be well-pleasing, not argumentative, not pilfering...to deny ungodliness and worldly desires and to live sensibly, righteously and godly in the present age (Titus 2:7-10,12 NASB).*

Whether artist or astronaut, surgeon or sailor, teacher or truck driver, aren't these attributes exactly what you want for your sons and daughters?

What about you?

Did your father push (or prompt) you into your career? Consider the influence he had on your schooling and vocation. Thank him. Or make peace with that decision. And, if a God-given yearning is stirred, consider a second career—perhaps in the Lord's work.

READY, SET, BUILD

"Put your outdoor work in order and get your fields ready; after that, build your house."

PROVERBS 24:27

Read that verse about four times. Okay? Now tell me—according to Proverbs—which is more important: preparing your fields or building your house?

Maybe it's saying, "Finish every bit of your work and only then—if there's time—take care of your family."

Or maybe it's saying, "Get your work out of the way as efficiently as possible, because more important work is waiting for you at home."

Or maybe it's saying, "Find time for work and family every day."

Or—if you consider the idea of completed action—you'll see that the work is not finished (it's only organized) and the fields are not harvested (they're only prepared), but the house is completed. It's built!

Or maybe it's just instructions to general contractors reminding them to consider things like soil composition and drainage before pouring a foundation and erecting stud walls.

I've got no answers to these questions. If the meaning of this passage keeps you awake at night, you could certainly ask your pastor. Or bring it up at your men's group. Or ask your bride.

How about this? Ask your kids. Say, "I came across this proverb in my devotional and I'm not sure how to take it. What do you think?"

If they respond with interest, that's fantastic. Read it out loud. Read it in context with other verses. See if you can find other Scripture passages that support one point of view.

All the while you won't just be answering one theological question. You'll be equipping your kids to be Bible-savvy for the rest of their lives.

What about you?

Isn't Bible study cool? Exploring God's Word and God's heart. I don't think the Bible is purposefully confusing. I think God wants us to mull it over, kick it around, and share it with others.

YOUR CHOICE, DAD

"There are times when parenthood seems like nothing but feeding the mouth that bites you."

PETER DE VRIES

Every time your teenager walks into the room you have two choices. You can let them know you are glad to see them. Or you can wonder what nastiness they have been up to and pick a fight.

If your body language is welcoming, if your smile is sincere, and if there's a plate of fudge on the kitchen counter, there's a good chance the interaction and conversation will be a positive experience. You may even get more than grunts and shrugs. Especially if you tell them a bit about your day and bring up something in which they find amusement or have a passing interest: the dog, the home team, your weird neighbors, a news story, an upcoming event, Grandma and Grandpa, vacation plans, the latest tech gadget, and so on.

If your body language repels, if your grimace is accusing, and if you're expecting bad news, then that's what you'll get. The first words out of your mouth should not be reminders of unfinished chores, accusations about dirty dishes or empty gas tanks, snide comparisons to perfect cousins, or queries about grades and homework.

In one case, they'll come in and plop down in your proximity because your companionship is tolerable for a short period of time. You may even learn something about their day.

In the other case, they'll schlep through or sneak past straight to their room. They are well aware that if they stop they'll somehow be in trouble for something, even if they're just guilty of adolescence.

Your choice, Dad.

What about you?

Consider your last conversation with your kid. Did you pull them toward you or push them away? Is an apology in order?

THE BEST-LAID PLANS

"'I know the plans I have for you,' declares the LORD, 'plans to prosper you and not to harm you, plans to give you hope and a future.'"

JEREMIAH 29:11

An ongoing theme in this devotional for dads is that we need to help our kids discover God's plan for their life. In earlier pages we talked about Dad as archer helping his child aim at the right target. We talked about helping our kids run the one specific race marked out for them. We even confirmed that we need to "train up a child in the way he should go."

The lessons are true. But if we insist that our kids have the perfect predictable plan *before* they begin their life journey, they may never take a first step. The fear of getting it wrong can be paralyzing. Even worse, they may begin to believe that any minor mistake or miscalculation that takes them off that path will leave them without any direction at all.

So let's clarify. God does have a plan for us and for each of our children. And it's perfect. But we can't know it all. We see down the road just far enough. Why? Because there are future joys and sorrows that we couldn't handle right now. If we knew everything that waited around the next corner, or the next, or the next after that, we wouldn't take another step.

So what should we tell our kids? What instructions can we offer that eliminate the fear of failure or the worry that comes from not knowing every bump or pothole in the road of life? Try these gentle reminders: Seek his will. Trust. Make ongoing decisions based on what we read in the Bible, what he reveals to us in prayer, and what we hear from wise counselors who are also connected to God.

And always, remember, his plan is to give all of us hope and a prosperous future.

What about you?

One great way to take the fear out of the future for your children is to tell them stories from your own life. You've probably endured crushing disappointments that—looking back—actually worked out in your best interest. Share those stories.

LET'S WATCH OUR SHOW

"I find television to be very educating.
Every time somebody turns on the set,
I go in the other room and read a book."

GROUCHO MARX

Much has been said about the vast wasteland that is television. And considering the majority of content, any thinking individual would have to agree. "Reality TV" shows that have nothing to do with reality. Totally dysfunctional families elevated to a place of honor. Mocking talk-show hosts. Cartoons that are not child-friendly. Lots and lots of people who like the sound of their own voice, but say nothing worth saying.

Well, this recommendation is going to come as a shocker. Let's go back to that great verse about fathering from Deuteronomy. "Those commandments that I give you...talk about them when you *sit at home*." With each of your children, find a weekly TV show you can share together. That's right. Intentionally create time in front of the TV with your kids. Call it "our show."

It could be something they already watch, and you flop on the couch next to them and just say, "Can I join you?" Or you may want to do some research on their interests or favorite film genres, find a show, and say, "Hey, have you seen this?"

I'm not going to suggest any particular show, but there are four things to remember. Set your TV controls to record it each week so you can watch it at a time that works for both of you. Zip through commercials. If any content is alarming, talk about it openly and honestly. Finally, when your show is over, model the extraordinary act of turning off the TV.

What about you?

In many homes, TV is a father's enemy. It ushers in ungodly morals, distracts from positive influences, and divides families. While your kids are still under your influence, you can equip them with tools to make a lifetime of wise TV-viewing decisions. Which is usually leaving it off.

GOD CAN HANDLE IT

"Rejoice always, pray continually, give thanks in all circumstances; for this is God's will for you in Christ Jesus."

1 Thessalonians 5:16-18

Think of the cruddiest situation you've endured in the last decade.

Changing a stubborn tire without gloves, on an expressway in a blizzard with semitrailers sloshing slush on your behind? That's nothing.

Watching your 16-year-old son throw out boxes of baseball cards, tattered jerseys, and a dozen baseball caps after he gets cut from the high-school baseball team, and you just don't know what to say or do? That's a little harder.

How about sitting for hours on end with a friend whose daughter is dying of leukemia? That's almost impossible to imagine.

Then read 1 Thessalonians, chapter 5. Does it seem like a cruel joke? Be joyful? Give thanks? This is God's will? God wants me to pray?

It's human nature to sometimes think that God may not want to hear from you when nasty stuff is happening. He's in charge and you're ticked off. If you start talking to him, you might say some things you regret.

Well, go ahead—be ticked. God can handle it. But at the same time, also do what the verse says: Keep praying and giving thanks. You may not be happy on the surface, but see if you can find a deeper, sustaining joy.

Bottom line: Remember that there's stuff we may not understand in the moment. Our puny human minds can't possibly decipher God's blueprint for eternity. But we can trust that—as we take the long view—joy, prayer, and thanksgiving are in God's will for us.

What about you?

If you're slogging through a long bout of crud, this may be an especially tough concept. But don't turn your back on this biblical truth. Instead, start looking for ways that God is drawing you to himself. There's a good chance he has placed other believers in your immediate vicinity who have gone through the same thing. Seek them out. Not for a pity party, but for a victory celebration.

MORE WORTH THAN THEY'RE TROUBLE

"Never trust the advice of a man in difficulties."

Aesop

As a speaker, it's not a bad idea to see how other speakers speak. That's why, recently, I found myself at a parenting seminar uncomfortably watching some guy billed as an "internationally known expert." For about an hour, I witnessed him point fingers, wring his hands, agonize, accuse, and yell about the importance of reasserting parental authority and keeping your kids in line. The guy was occasionally entertaining, but his core message was mean-spirited and depressing.

Not once did I hear him talk about *the joy of fatherhood.* Not once did I get the idea that he actually found any satisfaction from spending time with his kids. He did talk about *tough* love. But not much about *unconditional* love.

I cannot recall any of his memorized jokes, but the punch lines all seemed to center on how kids are "more trouble than they're worth" or how today's teenagers and parents cannot possibly have a civil adult conversation about life, current events, weekend plans, college plans, friends, or hopes and dreams. The speaker characterized parenting as "us" against "them." To this so-called international parenting expert, parenthood is years of gruesome, torturous, thankless toil.

He didn't take questions, which is probably a good thing, because I might have said something I'd have regretted later. At the very least, I would have reminded him that Psalm 127 confirms that children are a gift from the Lord. Maybe next time.

What about you?

Of course, I recommend you seek out parenting books, events, and resources for dads. But don't necessarily believe or implement everything they say. Run any parenting advice through the filter of God's Word, other Christian dads, and your wife's maternal instinct. And tell your kids often how awesome they are and how glad you are to be their dad.

ATTITUDE OF ENTITLEMENT

"A sluggard's appetite is never filled, but the desires of the diligent are fully satisfied."

Proverbs 13:4

There's a nasty rumor going around that young people today are afraid of a little hard work. They don't want to get their hands dirty. They have an attitude of entitlement. They want something for nothing.

I'm not sure if that rumor is true, but you have to admit it's out there. We can speculate where the idea comes from:

- The parents of today's teenagers (you and me) are one, maybe two, generations away from the Great Depression. We heard the stories and have an inkling of what it might have been like for much of the country to go to bed hungry. Our kids have never heard these stories.
- Fewer high-school kids have afterschool and summer jobs. There are so many extra-curricular activities available, and genuine commitment to a sport requires months

of out-of-season training. Teens work hard at their after-school activities, but they just don't have time for employment.

- Jobs around the house—lawn mowing, painting, housecleaning, even snow and leaf removal—are being hired out. Kids are rarely expected to work.
- In an attempt to keep up with other families, parents buy whatever their kids need or want. There's no motivation to save or get a job.
- Smaller families and divorced families are changing the financial dynamics when compared to past generations.
- Technology keeps kids inside, making them only appear lazy.

The point? As with many of the devotions in this book, see if you can use this idea to launch a dialogue with your kids. Plop down next to your teen on the couch and ask, "Are you a slug or do you just appear to be one?"

What about you?

Often it's easier to do a household task yourself than involve a young "helper." Your kids need to get off the couch and pull their weight. The trick is to make that happen without nagging.

LEAVING AND CLEAVING

"Where does the family start? It starts with a young man falling in love with a girl—no superior alternative has yet been found."

Sir Winston Churchill

Dad, the big day may be years away, but you've already thought about the day you get to walk your little girl down the aisle. Don't do anything that's going to mess that up.

When your precious daughter brings home a reasonably non-crazy and non-drooling young man, don't chase him away. (Even if he's a starving artist with a lip ring.) Because he may be the one. Don't divorce your wife, because she may remarry and your daughter would likely walk down the aisle alone rather than be forced to choose between her dear father and her dear stepdad. Do be ready to pay for at least some of the festivities.

Dad, when your son starts to think about sowing his wild oats, encourage him to take it slow. As a matter of fact, tell him flat-out to wait, wait, wait. If he's going too far too fast, he's going to have some physical, emotional, and spiritual regrets. Tell him the perfect bride is waiting for him. He needs to wait too.

Talk with your kids about God's plan for marriage.

And why it works. Explain that marriage is not a business relationship, legal contract, or a stage of life that happens for convenience or by accident. The second chapter in the Bible spells it out: "A man leaves his father and mother and is united to his wife, and they become one flesh" (Genesis 2:24).

Tell your kids that the idea of "two becoming one" is not a metaphor or cute saying. It really is God's plan for marriage.

And have that talk early and often. Way before they start dating.

What about you?

Are you loving your wife the way she needs to be loved? Forsaking all others. United. As one flesh.

ALONGSIDE GREATNESS

"If you want to build a ship, don't drum up the men to gather wood, divide the work, and give orders. Instead, teach them to yearn for the vast and endless sea."

Antoine de Saint-Exupéry

If you want your children to do great things, don't crush their spirits or overanalyze every performance. Don't overwhelm them with your brilliant insight before they even get off the ground.

If they're running for class president, don't criticize the font on their flyers. If they're nervous about a clarinet solo, don't remind them of their squeaky performance back in fourth grade. If they're in a cross-country meet the next morning, don't nag them to carb up or ask them which state-ranked runners they're competing against. They already know all that.

If your kids are investing themselves in meaningful activities, the last thing they need is a dad who points out every imperfection and potential stumbling block.

What they need is a parent who comes alongside them—figuratively or literally—and shares a vision of vast and endless possibilities. Make yourself available, but stay neutral. "I'm headed out to the store—do you need anything?" is a lot more helpful than "I just know you'll win" or "Don't get your hopes up."

If they're dreaming big things, dream right along with them. Don't be a dream-dasher or a dream-accelerator. If they ask for help, ease your way into the project. Proofread that term paper, don't rewrite it. Take the poster to the printer, don't redesign it. Video a practice session so they can critique themselves. Lend them a few file folders so they can organize themselves. Surprise them with a new tool, instrument, or app. Make sure the Gatorade is on ice.

Through it all, pray Psalm 90 for them and with them.

May the favor of the Lord our God rest on us; establish the work of our hands for us—yes, establish the work of our hands (Psalm 90:16-17).

What about you?

With God's guidance, your children have a real chance to do great things. Your job is to clear the way. Not necessarily lead the way. And definitely not get in the way.

THE GAME OF LIFE

"When a great adventure is offered, you don't refuse it."

AMELIA EARHART

The phrase "parenting is hard work" is one of those glib mantras that rolls off your tongue and lets you off the hook. It's part whine. Part excuse. Part easy answer when your kids are messing up and you don't know what to do.

Yikes.

Let me be clear. Does being a dad take time? Yes. Lots of it.

Are there moments when you have to use every ounce of your brainpower and expend great physical energy to meet a challenge presented by one of your kids? Yes.

Do you have to decipher clues about what makes each of your children tick, coordinate strategies with your children's mother, share tactics with other dads, read books, go to seminars, and pray fervently? Yes.

But is it work? No.

Instead, think of it as a quest. A puzzle. Being a father is a journey of discovery and wonderment. When your family is together, it's the ultimate mystery party game.

If you accept the challenge, commit to the adventure, and pursue wise solutions, then great rewards will come early and often. And Dad, if you stay in the game, focusing on the heart of the matter (the hearts of your kids), the rewards keep coming for the rest of your life.

A word of warning: Next time you hear someone say, "Parenting is hard work," you probably should not launch into a nasty rant. Instead say, "Yeah. Parenting might not be easy. But every effort you put into it comes back a hundred times."

What about you?

Working hard to be the kind of dad your kids need? Keep at it. Your effort will not go unnoticed.

LOVING LAWS

"I do not understand what I do. For what I want to do I do not do, but what I hate I do."

ROMANS 7:15

Show of hands. Anyone struggling with sin?

Well, that proves you're human. Plus, there's a sense in which your struggle is good news. How's that? Because only true believers struggle with sin. If you're not a believer then you don't worry about such minor details.

When you have time, read all of Romans, chapter 7. It will help you understand how the law doesn't cause you to sin—it just makes you aware of your shortcomings. The law gives you a formula for avoiding sin and all the crud that follows. But only Jesus can break the bondage of sin. Keeping the law doesn't save us. Even if we could somehow never do anything outwardly wrong, our hearts and minds still betray us.

Romans 7 never really mentions anything about parents and children, but we can still draw some insights for fathers. Our kids are also struggling with sin. They are going to break God's rules and our house rules. We shouldn't fear it; we should expect it. When our kids miss curfew, trash talk, gossip, sneak a beer, whine about the neighbor's new flat screen, or deceive us about their destination for their evening, our response should not be to change the rules or to let them off the hook. The law doesn't change. But their transgression should lead to a discussion (or maybe a lecture) on why rules are good things. Plus an appropriate punishment.

Later in Romans 7 we read, "I delight in God's law" (Romans 7:22). One of the benefits of parenthood is finally understanding that verse.

What about you?

One great thing about parenting is that you are forced to think about the many truths and principles your children need to know. For better or worse, you get to apply them to your own life as well.

I MISS YOU, DAD

"You can't do anything about the length of your life, but you can do something about its width and depth."

Evan Esar

When your father passes away, the funeral director will offer to write a short obituary. Instead, I recommend you volunteer for the task. I did.

You see, right in the middle of my work on the manuscript for this devotional for dads, my own dad died. I set aside this project for a few days. When I finally came back, it seemed trivial. But also more important than ever.

My dad—Ken Payleitner—was a World War II vet, an elementary school principal for 32 years, and a loving patriarch to his family of four children, eleven grandchildren, and even two great-grandkids. My dad and mom were married for 61 years. At first, I thought that was all that needed to be said.

But then I started digging. Digging up stories from Dad's old students and teachers on his staff—stories I had never heard before. Then searching my own personal memory bank, I recalled how Dad had always been there at critical junctions in my life: during educational, career, and spiritual turning points, often helping turn occasions of disappointment into opportunities for growth.

A few days later, standing in line at the funeral home shaking hands, I found myself looking into the eyes of scores of people who kept repeating things like, "Your father was a wonderful man" and "Your dad was important to me." Writing that obit helped me understand their accolades. I could smile through the tears.

Not surprisingly, the process of writing his obit became one last challenge from my dad—a challenge to work even harder on my own legacy.

What about you?

What will your son or daughter write in your obituary? Or say at your funeral? If that thought makes you uncomfortable, I recommend you join me and start putting together a plan that will add a few positive paragraphs to what they might write or say.

SPONTANEOUS CONSUMPTION

"Your wife will be like a fruitful vine within your house; your children will be like olive shoots around your table."

Psalm 128:3

We were having an impromptu family gathering. Ten of us, and I was the patriarch. My four sons, one daughter, and three daughters-in-law. Alec, Lindsay, Randall, Rachel, Max, Megan, Isaac, Rae Anne.

Rita and I normally enjoy planning a menu for such events. But this one had come together spontaneously in the last hours of a busy week. I had an idea. We all jumped in two cars and drove to the local specialty supermarket. We swarmed the aisles and came away with $117 of food. (Plus a sock monkey.)

The only rule was that anything you put in the cart stays in the cart and goes through the checkout line. (Including sock monkeys.)

The final menu: Steaks. Cannoli. Tiramisu. Carrot cake mix. Frosting. Salad fixin's. Chips. Lemonade. Raspberry lemonade. Macaroni salad. Sour Patch straws. Guacamole. Salsa. Bottled cherry soda. Awesome bread. Slider buns. Horseradish. All in all, a tasty spread. (Except for the sock monkey.)

The crowded prep in the kitchen added to the spontaneity of the day. The rib eyes were grilled to perfection. The meal was surprisingly balanced. And every one cleaned up! The final cost was actually less than taking the crew to most restaurants.

I tell this story for three reasons. One, it's fun for me to tell and relive the day. Two, it's a reminder that God wants us to bring our family together in celebration. Three, I hope you'll try creative group grocery-shopping. It's a spontaneous and amusing way to spend an afternoon and share a meal with your older children, their spouses, and friends. (Including sock monkeys.)

What about you?

Quite a few dads need to develop their capacity to go with the flow. Orchestrate moments for your kids to be creative, and then stay back and watch them do some silly, awesome, and priceless memory-making.

AS I UNDERSTAND IT

"It ain't those parts of the Bible that I can't understand that bother me, it is the parts that I do understand."

MARK TWAIN

Some of Scripture is just plain difficult to comprehend. There are parts that scholars and theologians debate with sincerity and ferocity. Sometimes I listen and try to follow. Most of the time I am content to just major on the majors and let the PhDs hash out the stuff that isn't fundamental to the eternal destiny of me or my kids.

Here's what I do know. Nobody's perfect. We're all sinners. Because of that we're not worthy to hang out with God. Death is inevitable. When I die somebody has to pay for my sin. If it's me, I guess I am going to hell just as I deserve. Thankfully, there's a way out. God sent his only Son to live on earth and pay the price for my sins (and yours) on the cross. Best of all, that ticket to heaven cost me nothing. (Same for you.) I just have to understand it and accept that gift.

I'm thinking that Mark Twain was a smart, well-read guy. He understood all this too. I'm hoping that he was joking about being bothered about sin and salvation. Because I would sure love to hang out with him on the other side of eternity.

What about you?

Without directly quoting Scripture, I just laid out the plan of salvation and recited the sinner's prayer. Do you see how it doesn't take fancy words to spell it out? Like Mark Twain, I'm hoping to see you there too. And your kids.

RITE OF PASSAGE

"Then [Jacob] blessed Joseph and said, 'May the God before whom my fathers Abraham and Isaac walked faithfully, the God who has been my shepherd all my life to this day, the Angel who has delivered me from all harm—may he bless these boys. May they be called by my name and the names of my fathers Abraham and Isaac, and may they increase greatly on the earth.'"

GENESIS 48:15-16

A few years back, Gary Smalley and John Trent wrote a book titled *The Blessing*, and more recently Jim McBride wrote a very practical book, *Rite of Passage*.

The books—backed up with biblical examples—suggest that dads be intentional about creating a moment in time or even a ceremony in which we tell our children one at a time, "You are my beloved child. These are your gifts. This is what matters. Here are a handful of truths to hold on to. I am so proud of you." This blessing would include ideas specific to that child as well as universal principles relevant to all growing Christians.

To be sure, those words and feelings need to be part of everyday life. But delivering them with intentionality as your son or daughter approaches adulthood can give them a foundation upon which they can build for the rest of their life.

Of course, a "rite of passage" can be anything from a two-person walk in the woods to an elaborate ritual involving a host of mentors, symbolic gifts, and a keepsake guidebook for life filled with letters and quotations. It could be an hour or a weekend.

Sound over the top? Not at all. Sound like a lot of work? Perhaps. But think about the impression it will have on your young teenager. Forever.

What about you?

When did you know you were an adult? It probably had something to do with your father. Something he said. A responsibility he gave to you. Maybe something he stopped doing because he knew you could do it yourself. It may have been his handshake the day you stopped living under his roof. Remember to make the most of those moments with your sons and daughters.

GET IN THE GAME

"Sports don't build character; they reveal it."

John Wooden

Get your kids involved in traveling baseball, softball, soccer, track, volleyball, wrestling, gymnastics, ice skating, hockey, basketball, lacrosse, fencing, golf, archery, cheerleading, and so on.

Are you surprised by such a recommendation in a men's devotional? That's because traveling sports have been getting an unjustified bad rap these days from some pastors and church leaders. We're told that traveling sports are a distraction from Sunday-morning church and that kids can't handle the high expectations and time commitment. I guess that's possible. But that's being regrettably shortsighted.

The benefits of having a child over 12 on a traveling team with rigorous demands and an occasional overnight tournament are incalculable. What can they learn? Perseverance, self-denial, hard work, sacrifice, dedication, organization, and respect for authority. Plus teamwork, making tough choices, leadership, winning with humility, and losing with grace. All under your watchful eye.

Plus, in the car and between events, your young athlete is spending one-on-one time with you. The long drives and overnights lead to significant memories and life-changing conversations. Those sometimes grueling trips served as rites of passage for all my kids.

Did we miss some Sunday-morning services at our home church? Of course. We talked about that choice. We talked about legalism and grace. Together we acknowledged and honored the Sabbath. My kids also sacrificed some youth-group activities. But they remained committed to their teams, often seeing them as a mission field. They modeled the Christian life on and off the field. They boldly stood their ground with unchurched teammates, something they never would have experienced sitting passively in a church rec room surrounded by other youth-group members.

The wins and losses have blurred with time. But the investment of time and money in traveling sports was worth every nickel and every hour.

What about you?

Don't force your kids into sports. But if they commit, you commit 110 percent. Following them through their high-school and college athletic careers, you'll be able to make a direct connection between their early successes and later opportunities.

A LOOK WORTH TAKING

"Fathers, do not exasperate your children; instead, bring them up in the training and instruction of the Lord."

EPHESIANS 6:4

Ephesians 6:4 features a negative and positive command.

The positive is straightforward. Practically speaking, training and instructing your offspring in the ways of the Lord probably includes getting to church on Sunday mornings, finishing each day with bedtime prayers, carpooling to Awana or some other weekly kids' church activity, being creative and faithful with family devotions, and filling your home with videos, music downloads, CDs, and books that deliver biblical truths in a way that is attractive and applicable to your children. Plus presenting your own life as a model for following Christ.

The negative side of the equation is perhaps more difficult for fathers to assess. Sometimes dads do things that exasperate their children and we don't even know it. The following list of questions is not accusatory, but is offered as a public service so that you might consider the possible darker side of your personality.

Do you use sarcasm or mocking tones? Are you

quick to judge without getting all the facts? Do you have low expectations for your kids? Or are your expectations too high? Do you push your kids to do what you couldn't? Are you a jerk in the stands? Do you abuse alcohol? Do you break promises? Are you gone for days at a time without checking in? Do you lecture without listening? Do you lie? Do you deny freedoms? Do you hold grudges? Do you threaten or give ridiculous ultimatums? Do you call them names?

Sorry about all these images. It's really no fun at all to consider such things. But I have one more. Do you do any of the above, not to your kids...but to their mother?

All dads need to heed both sides of the Ephesians 6:4 equation. Every dad is different. But no kid deserves to be exasperated.

What about you?

In what way did your father exasperate you? As you assess the above list you may want to consider those traits first.

LIVING SACRIFICES

"I urge you, brothers and sisters, in view of God's mercy, to offer your bodies as a living sacrifice, holy and pleasing to God—this is your true and proper worship. Do not conform to the pattern of this world, but be transformed by the renewing of your mind. Then you will be able to test and approve what God's will is—his good, pleasing and perfect will."

Romans 12:1-2

Got a son or daughter who drinks alcohol, smokes pot or cigarettes, sniffs glue, huffs, dips, does hard drugs, or cuts themselves?

I am not an expert. But I do know this. When they were little, they trusted you to feed them, keep them safe, tuck them in, and keep the monsters out of the closet. Today, they still trust you to keep them safe and keep the monsters away.

So do whatever it takes. Get help. Talk to experts. Involve other adults they have trusted and respected in the past. Do research. If necessary, search their room, their car, and their clothes. Inspect their purses and wallets. Hack into their e-mail and social media conversations. Don't jump to conclusions, but make well-reasoned conclusions. If their life is in danger, don't worry about breaking their trust. They trust you to protect them. Consider a professionally led intervention.

Pray Romans 12 for them. Several times per day. Like this, "Heavenly Father, in view of God's mercy, I lift up Ashley as a living sacrifice. Help her life to be holy and pleasing to you, God, as a true and proper act of worship. Help her conform not to the pattern of the world, but be transformed by the renewing of her mind. Help Ashley to be able to test and approve your will—your good, pleasing, and perfect will."

At the right time, tell your child that you are praying for them. Even ask if you can pray *with* them.

Keep loving them. Don't hate them. Hate what they're doing.

What about you?

Are you offering your own body as a living sacrifice, holy and pleasing to God?

FROM BELIEF TO FAITH

"The longest journey a man must take is the eighteen inches from his head to his heart."

UNKNOWN

Periodically, steer conversations with your children to spiritual matters. You need to see where they are. You need to see what they believe. Don't bash them over the head, but take advantage of opportunities that come up after church, at the dinner table, and during quiet moments when it's just the two of you.

When the topic of belief versus faith comes up, here's a great story to tell.

> *A hundred years ago or so, a tightrope walker drew cheers from an appreciative crowd by confidently crossing over Niagara Falls on a rope. He asked the onlookers, "Now, do you believe I can push a wheelbarrow across and back?" They cheered even louder as he made that trip without hesitation. Then he asked, "Now, do you believe I can push this wheelbarrow across and back with someone riding inside?" They cheered wildly. He yelled over the roar, "Who will volunteer?" The crowd became very quiet.*

That's a pretty good illustration of the difference between belief and faith. The crowd believed the tightrope walker could do it. Intellectually, they were right with him. But they didn't have enough faith to trust him with their lives. The difference was that their heart could not accept what their brain had seen.

The Bible tells us that "it is with your heart that you believe and are justified" (Romans 10:10).

What about you?

Adult men sometimes have the hardest time with this. We like to address any and all convictions "head first." But we also have to surrender our hearts. Ask yourself and your kids if you pass the test of Romans 10:10.

WHO ARE YOU?

"Apart from Jesus Christ we cannot know the meaning of our life or our death, of God or of ourselves."

BLAISE PASCAL

You meet another guy at a golf outing, fund-raising event, or standing on the sidelines of a youth soccer game. You make small talk and then he says, "Tell me a little about yourself." What's the first thing you mention? Your job, right? "I'm an electrical engineer." "I'm a paleontologist." "I'm in marketing." You may go on for another sentence or two describing where or how long, or even what you'd rather be doing. Only as an afterthought do you add, "Oh yeah—I've got a wife and three kids."

Is that really who you are? Is that your identity? If your son or daughter were standing next to you, would you at least identify yourself as a family man before your career? Would your initial response be something like, "I've got a beautiful wife of 15 years, three kids, and a dog named Beaker"?

Well, that's better. Except the dog gets named and your family members don't. Let's read Galatians 2:20 and then try again.

I have been crucified with Christ and I no longer live, but Christ lives in me. The life I live in the body, I live by faith in the Son of God, who loved me and gave himself for me (Galatians 2:20).

The idea is to put your most important identity first. Yes, your bride is hot, your kids are perfect, you're a scratch golfer, your dogs are blue-ribbon holders, and you retired a multimillionaire at 36 before the economy went bad. But first and foremost you are a believer. Right?

So try this: "I'm a follower of Jesus Christ, a husband, a father, and a championship NASCAR driver." You get the idea. We need to put first things first. Really, the words we say are not nearly as important as the attitude of our heart.

What about you?

If your identity is "in Christ," then the people with whom you regularly come in contact should know that. When put into practice, small talk about your work life may actually be the best place to start a conversation with a stranger.

HISTORY LESSONS

"Encourage the young men to be self-controlled. In everything set them an example by doing what is good. In your teaching show integrity, seriousness and soundness of speech that cannot be condemned, so that those who oppose you may be ashamed because they have nothing bad to say about us."

Titus 2:6-8

Dads, what are your most vivid memories from your youth? Were you a hippie? A punk rocker? Did you disco in the 1970s? Did you break-dance in the '80s? Did you vogue or grind in the 1990s? Did you get a Walkman for Christmas? A boombox? Did you have one of the first Macintosh computers? Did you skateboard or Rollerblade? What was your first car? A used Gremlin? Pinto? AMC Pacer? Did you watch those ridiculous sitcoms like *Three's Company*, *Family Ties*, and *Facts of Life*? Did you own light-up sneakers, a jean jacket, Ray-Ban sunglasses, or platform shoes? Did you waste hours playing Super Mario Brothers or Pac-Man? Did you have a mullet, a rattail, a Mohawk, or huge sideburns? What historic events mark your youth? Watergate? The fall of the Berlin Wall? Mount St. Helens? Chernobyl? The space shuttle *Challenger* disintegrating 73 seconds after launch? The Columbine shooting? September 11?

Those are more than memories. Those are points of connection to the next generation. If you mention some of this stuff, are you afraid your kids would roll their eyes? That's the idea! That gives you total permission to roll your eyes and groan at some of their choices.

Talking about the past choices you made and the ones you regret is a great parenting strategy. You may be afraid they'll use it against you, but just the opposite is true. They can learn from your mistakes and maybe even seek out your advice. Considering historic and cultural touch points gives them context for your world and theirs.

What about you?

In your youth, don't you remember being amused by stories told by your parents or your aunts and uncles? There's something weirdly provocative about considering what your mom and dad were like when they were your age. Take advantage of that curiosity to connect with your kids.

THE MORE GOLDEN RULE

"Do to others as you would have them do to you."

Luke 6:31

This is actually just plain good advice. As a matter of fact, they say that all the world's major religions have some version of the Golden Rule someplace in their sacred writings.

Doing good to others is smart life strategy, but it's not a particularly impressive spiritual feat. Being nice to your boss increases the chance for a promotion. Being nice to your kid's soccer coach may increase their playing time. Being nice at a fast-food restaurant decreases the chance they spit in your milkshake. A few verses down in Luke's Gospel is a clear reminder that doing "good to those who are good to you" is not considered heroic because "even sinners do that" (Luke 6:33).

However, there are two ways to turn "doing good" into a significant spiritual act. But they take a little extra effort. One is the challenge to "love your enemies, do good to them" (Luke 6:35). That's a little tougher, isn't it? The other is to do your good works in secret. This verse in Matthew explains it well:

> *When you give to the needy, do not let your left hand know what your right hand is doing, so that*

your giving may be in secret. Then your Father, who sees what is done in secret, will reward you (Matthew 6:3-4).

Ever hear someone say, "All religions are the same. They all have the 'Golden Rule'"? Next time respond by saying, "The Golden Rule is easy—for the most part it's self-serving. I suggest you try reading and living the rest of the gospel."

What about you?

Dad, don't just live by the Golden Rule and stop there. Be good to your enemy. Do good deeds in secret. That will get your children's attention.

DEADLINES AND DEAD AIR

"Time is the coin of your life. It is the only coin you have, and only you can determine how it will be spent. Be careful lest you let other people spend it for you."

CARL SANDBURG

As a veteran radio producer, I have deadlines that must be met—daily, weekly, monthly. If I drop the ball, radio stations across the country play dead air, and no one is happy about that. My clients lose media airtime. The stations look foolish. Listeners are shaking their radios wondering why they've suddenly gone silent.

Early in my career, I was nice and polite, giving out deadlines that often left me scrambling to play catch-up. I didn't leave any dead air, but I did work some late nights, snap at people I cared about, and interrupt other work to take care of last-minute snags and tweaks. What should have been routine revisions became emergencies because of a can't-miss deadline.

Most guys would have figured this out very quickly, but it took me several years. When I moved all the deadlines up by two weeks, then suddenly all the last-minute panic went away. All the people involved (including me) could take a long weekend, take a sick day, survive a computer crash, or work efficiently on other projects without causing a boatload of stress.

You may not be in the radio business, but you certainly have people you count on and people who count on you—at work and at home. I recommend you reconsider all your deadlines and start earlier—a minute, a week, a month, a year. Life will be easier on you, your wife, and your kids. Once in a while you'll still have some last-minute stress-filled deadlines, but instead of being the goat, you'll be the hero for coming to the rescue.

What about you?

Time management is referenced frequently in Scripture, but usually referring to the idea that we only have a short time on earth to tell others about Jesus. See Colossians 4:5, James 4:13-15, and 1 Corinthians 7:29. That's one deadline you definitely don't want to miss. In the meantime, a little margin in your life can lead to a less-stressed dad and closer families.

FOR GOOD OR EVIL

"I think that technologies are morally neutral until we apply them. It's only when we use them for good or for evil that they become good or evil."

William Gibson

The Internet is not your enemy. It may seem otherwise, but technology should not get credit or blame for how it is used. When naked women show up regularly on your laptop, it's not the fault of the World Wide Web. When following your friends and *their* friends distracts you from productive work for an entire afternoon, it's not the fault of Facebook or Google. When you rear-end the car in front of you, it's not the fault of Sprint, AT&T, or Verizon.

Dad, you need to accept responsibility for how you use all the amazing technology available today. And teach your kids to do the same.

As a matter of fact, here's one example of how social media can be used for good.

My daughter, Rae Anne, sent a mass text to her immediate family members from her barracks at West Point. It was a simple request to "throw up a quick prayer" for a math test coming up that afternoon. A few minutes later, a one-word response popped up from my wife, Rita: "Done." From his office in Chicago, my son

Randall followed with another text: "Done." Daughter-in-law Megan texted from her classroom, "Done." I smiled, prayed, and did the same. In a matter of minutes, six family members prayed for Rae Anne and her math test 800 miles away.

For that chain of events, I would be glad to take full responsibility. But I can't. I'm still learning how to use all this fancy-schmancy technical stuff. Often, I just follow my kids' lead.

Oh yeah, another text later that week reported that on that math test, Rae Anne did "pretty well."

What about you?

There are a lot of inventions—books, cars, movies, guns, pharmaceuticals—that are really morally neutral. We have the choice to use them for good or evil. Take responsibility, Dad.

THE TRADITION TEST

"If any of you lacks wisdom, you should ask God, who gives generously to all without finding fault, and it will be given to you."

James 1:5

Did you ever unintentionally overlook a family tradition?

Maybe you forgot the yams at Thanksgiving. You decided not to go see the Christmas lights because the weather was bad. You put a new angel on top of the tree. Did you notice who gets the most upset about a lost tradition? It's the teenagers in the family. They'll say things like, "We have to! We've always done it that way."

Then the next holiday comes around and those same teenagers are mocking some other tradition. "Omigosh, that is so lame. I can't believe you still expect us to do that." Or they will totally ignore some other cherished family tradition. "Why would we watch fireworks from the Feeneys' backyard when the Potters have a much better view?"

Stuck between childhood freedom and adult responsibility, young people crave traditions to give them stability and roots. At the same time, they also are trying out their sprouting wings. Every day brings new discoveries and new options. From a father's perspective, it's an amazing, jaw-clenching, and fulfilling process to watch.

I don't usually recommend that parents give in to teenage demands, but this may be the exception. When they insist on keeping a tradition, give in. When they suggest a new way of doing things, give in. Next year is another story.

What about you?

As with so many phases of our growing children, we need to expect teenagers to assert their independence and challenge our authority. It's the classic time-honored quest for wisdom. As modeled by God, we need to give generously without finding fault. So be ready, Dad. Not with an iron fist, but an understanding heart.

THE NEXT VERSE

"The thief comes only to steal and kill and destroy; I came that they may have life, and have it abundantly."

John 10:10 NASB

This happens all the time in Scripture. You read something that makes you feel one way. And then the very next verse or phrase flips it around.

Reading the first part of John 10:10, you can't help but say, "How can I stop Satan's thievery?" You don't have to wait long to read the secret to abundant life: Jesus came.

"All have sinned and fall short of the glory of God" is a sad reality. But the next verse gives us God's plan for redemption: "All are justified freely by his grace through the redemption that came by Christ Jesus" (Romans 3:23-24).

The fifth commandment starts with something that's not always easy. "Honor your father and mother." But the payoff is a promise. "Then you will live a long, full life in the land the Lord your God is giving you" (Exodus 20:12 NLT).

You remember Jesus' comforting words in Matthew 11:28? "Come to me, all of you who are weary and carry heavy burdens, and I will give you rest" (NASB). The next verse starts with five words that don't sound like rest: "Take my yoke upon you" (Matthew 11:29 NLT).

Dad, if these examples were intriguing to you, share them with your kids. Be their trail guide for the adventurous expedition of reading God's Word.

What about you?

Every day something interesting or amusing crosses your mind or your path. How often do you share it with your kids? Give them a chance—they may start sharing their discoveries with you.

ONCE IS FUNNY

"...a time to weep and a time to laugh."

—Ecclesiastes 3:4

I love to laugh with my kids. Don't you? It feels good just being goofy. But sometimes it goes too far. Kids don't always know when to stop. Honestly, I'm amused when my kids jump on me when I'm reading the paper, put ice down my back, or turn the lights off when I'm in the basement. It's a joke, I get it. Once.

The problem is that a five-year-old thinks that if it was good for a laugh one time, then it should work again and again. They have not embraced the truth of Proverbs 15:20. It says, "Sensible children bring joy to their father" (Proverbs 15:20 NLT). Our kids get the *joy* part, but they often miss the *sensible* part of that verse.

How do you get them to understand that less is more? That you can have too much of a good thing? Dad, sometimes we need to be a parent instead of a playmate. You can't punish them. What they did isn't wrong. It's just gone on a bit too long. So you get them quiet and say, "That's enough. Once is funny." Those words—"Once is funny"—get everyone off the hook. You've still had a good laugh together, but when you don't laugh the second time, you're not being hypocritical. You're just showing that there's a time and place, a need for judgment.

I think kids can understand how that, sometimes, "once is funny." It also works well for the occasional bit of gross-out humor that crops up. You can't help but laugh when the baby burps at the dinner table, but when the older kids repeat the noise, those three words can put a stop to it.

So don't ever stifle a chuckle when you're with your children. You can always cover yourself by saying, "Hey, kids we've all had a good laugh now. But, once is funny."

What about you?

"Once is funny" is one of those great phrases to tuck in your fathering toolbox. If you have any that work well for you, pass them on to other dads. I'd also love to add it to my collection. Track me down at jaypayleitner.com.

THE WAGES OF SIN

"If the Son sets you free, you will be free indeed."

John 8:36

Does life have you feeling trapped, stuck in a rut, or not living up to your expectations? It's fashionable to blame God—but don't. Very likely, your rut can be traced back to a sin problem. Jesus told his disciples, "I tell you the truth, everyone who sins is a slave of sin" (John 8:34 NLT).

Examples of sin that leads to enslavement are easy to come up with:

- Someone with a habit of lying will spend a lot of time lying to cover up the original lies. And worrying about getting caught.
- Sex outside of marriage opens the door to all kinds of diseases, to unwanted pregnancies, and to suspicions, worries, and intimacy issues with your spouse or future spouse.
- Being envious of your neighbor's stuff leads to a life chasing things that inevitably leave you with a stack of credit-card debt and an empty heart.
- Dishonor your parents and Thanksgiving

gatherings are destined to be filled with bitterness and ill will. Or empty chairs.

Let your kids know that sin takes the joy from life. Give them real-world examples they can relate to. You may have already taught your kids that—in the scope of eternity—"the wages of sin is death" (Romans 6:23). Shouldn't they also be made aware of the consequences of sin here on earth?

Following Christ sets us free to enjoy his unlimited, unconditional love. Both here and in the hereafter.

What about you?

You can easily come up with several examples of sin and bad choices in your own life. Some had immediate consequences. Some had long-term consequences. Some, though not all of them, should be shared with your children as lessons learned the hard way.

FEAR NOT

"Do what you are afraid to do."

Ralph Waldo Emerson

I won't rat them out by name. But one of my kids has a fear of snakes and one has a fear of spiders. They don't stay locked shivering in their rooms, so it's not a paralyzing problem. My wife, Rita, has a bit of acrophobia, so I'm sure I won't be taking her mountain climbing anytime soon.

There's nothing really wrong or unhealthy about most fears. Actually, we want our younger children to be a little afraid of crossing the street alone, eating mushrooms from the yard, and petting strange dogs.

Some kids, however, experience fears that are debilitating. Ambition is drained. Actions are repressed. Around every corner lurks a bogeyman or insurmountable challenge. When our kids are hurting, it's important that we don't just quote a Bible verse and say, "Get over it." Still, Scripture is always a good place to start.

> *The Lord himself goes before you and will be with you; he will never leave you nor forsake you. Do not be afraid; do not be discouraged (Deuteronomy 31:8).*

Peace I leave with you; my peace I give you. I do not give to you as the world gives. Do not let your hearts be troubled and do not be afraid (John 14:27).

So if God says to not be afraid, what should a dad say? As with most fathering challenges, you'll want to help your kids see all sides of an issue, take a short- and long-term view, and explore options. When it comes to childhood fears, the best thing is usually to come alongside and face them together. Use all your best fathering tools: logic, patience, respect, personal experience, confidence, and humor.

Whether the fear is short-lived or requires a professional counselor, the goal really is "Do not be afraid."

What about you?

Adult fears are usually a little more complex than childhood fears. Still, the goal remains the same. Accept Jesus' perfect love because "Perfect love casts out fear" (1 John 4:18 NASB).

WORTH THE TRIP

"A man travels the world in search of what he needs and returns home to find it."

George Moore

Grade-school kids love hanging out with Dad. That may not be the case in middle school. By high school, dads can feel marginalized in the life of their teenager. A season of disconnection and distance should not be a big surprise and isn't a reason for panic or overreaction. On the other hand, this might be the time to take drastic action.

What might that be? How about signing yourself and your young teen up for a weeklong mission trip? Appalachia. Haiti. Mexico. Russia. Wherever God is working. There's a good chance your church or another church in your area is planning a trip in the very near future.

Two words of advice. Make sure it's an actual mission trip that does real evangelization or real work to meet real needs, not just an excuse for a vacation. Also, make sure that the week you're gone is not critical to other plans your teen may have. Such as team tryouts, a special event, or something that they've been looking forward to for quite a while. Taking them out of school for a valuable learning experience such as this actually is not out of the question.

Bring it up. See what they say. Present it as a way to do something awesome, not as a plan to help you reconnect with them.

Last thought. Mission experiences with the entire family are worth the effort. But a dad spending a week working side by side with a coming-of-age son or daughter will lead to experiences and memories that will keep you on the same page and communicating openly for decades to come.

What about you?

Want to be amazed by the wisdom, strength, heart, and creativity of your own flesh and blood? Take them out of their comfort zone and turn them loose for Jesus.

THE MEANING OF LIFE

"A ship is safe in harbor,
but that's not what ships are for."

William Shedd

So your sharp young teenager is searching for the meaning of life. That's good. It's a lot better than letting life pass them by without a second thought.

In their quest for knowledge and purpose, they will probably read, surf, watch, dialogue, blog, tweet, and ponder deep thoughts. Eventually they may even come to their old dad for some insight from a more mature perspective. Will you be ready?

I hope you don't laugh at them. Think about how you would have felt—through your teen years and twenties—if your father had laughed at you when you came to him for wisdom.

What you can do is help them see the bigger picture. If a quiet moment presents itself, you may want to lower your voice and deliver this all-encompassing truth with quiet authority: "Son...daughter...it took me a while to learn this. And you may not believe this. But...it's not about you." If that stops the conversation, then you've left them with something to mull over. If conversation continues, you could pull out a portion or two of Scripture to support your point.

Whoever finds their life will lose it, and whoever loses their life for my sake will find it (Matthew 10:39).

Do nothing out of selfish ambition or vain conceit. Rather, in humility value others above yourselves (Philippians 2:3).

Jesus called the Twelve and said, "Anyone who wants to be first must be the very last, and the servant of all" (Mark 9:35).

It all comes back to surrendering to God's will, doesn't it? Our identity is not in who we are, but in who God is and how that shows up in our daily life.

What about you?

Dads spend a lot of time challenging their children to do great things. Maybe we need to spend more time defining what the word *great* really means.

WELL-WORN, WELL-READ

"Oh, how I love your law!
I meditate on it all day long."
PSALM 119:97

Here's a pretty accurate diagnostic tool for how you're doing in your personal faith journey. It's not 100 percent accurate, but it's an instructive indicator that things are going well in your pursuit to follow God's will for your life. Or whether you're falling a bit short.

Grab your personal study Bible—if you can find it—and assess its physical appearance. I submit that the condition of your personal faith journey is inversely proportional to the condition of your Bible. In other words, the more wear and tear on your Bible, the better.

Certainly, you need to respect the book itself and shouldn't abuse it. But you should feel comfortable interacting with it: opening it often, underlining passages, and writing notes in the margin. Hebrews 4:12 says "the word of God is living and active" (NASB). But if your Bible stays trapped in the dark of a bookshelf or the far, unreachable corner of a drawer in your desk, it has not had the chance to breathe truth into your life.

Please don't go judging your neighbor on the wear and tear of his Bible. His online Bible may get lots and lots of hits. He may be on a brand-new edition, having worn out five others in his lifetime. He may be a very delicate reader. Or he may be a new Christian about to embark on the extraordinary adventure of digging into God's Word for the first time.

An even bigger point to remember is this: Just reading the Bible doesn't cut it. What we read needs to impact how we think and what we do. "Do not merely listen to the word, and so deceive yourselves. Do what it says" (James 1:22).

Still, there's nothing comparable to a well-worn, well-read Bible.

What about you?

You know those comfy jeans you love so much. Your Bible should feel just that comfortable. Even when its challenges make you uncomfortable.

THE OPPOSITE OF A TOGA PARTY

"Noble fathers have noble children."

EURIPIDES

Noble. That's a great word. That's a great goal.

Breeze through the dictionary and you come across definitions like "distinguished by outstanding qualities and lofty character" and "possessing superiority of mind, ideals, and morals."

So where have all the noble people gone? Maybe it was easier to be noble in the fourth century BC. Can't you picture the ancient Greek playwright standing in his robe in a marble archway proclaiming ideas that are lofty and altruistic?

Looking at our fallen world today, I'm thinking most dads have given up the goal of raising noble children. I've heard fathers joke that they expect their kids to be screwed up, but they just hope they aren't as screwed up as the kids down the block. Has it come to that? Are we really going to settle for kids with no conscience or honor? Don't you want to raise kids of integrity, high ideals, and righteousness?

Maybe that five-word quote from Euripides gives us a hint about how to raise noble children. Well, there it is! Did you miss it? Noble fathers are the starting point. Noble children are the result. To get noble children, Dad, you need to get there yourself.

So for the sake of your kids, get your own heart right. You and your children will then have a shot at a noble life. But don't take just take the word of a Greek playwright. Psalm 97:11 promises, "Light shines on the righteous and joy on the upright in heart."

What about you?

Are you "distinguished by lofty character" and the possession of "superiority of mind, ideals, and morals"? Well, neither am I. But if you start working on that today, I promise I will too.

ALL YOU NEED IS A GOOD EDITOR

"For many of us the great danger is not that we will renounce our faith. It is that we will become so distracted and rushed and preoccupied that we will settle for a mediocre version of it."

JOHN ORTBERG

In the midst of our frantic, overloaded lives, we forget how good we have it. And when we forget how good we have it, then we forget to thank the Supplier. And when we forget to thank the Supplier, we start to think we've been doing it all on our own. And when we start to think we've been doing it all on our own, we stop seeking his—God's—will and guidance. And when we stop seeking his will and guidance, we end up doing our own thing. And when we do our own thing, it's never as good as what he had planned for us. Mediocrity is the result. A job that's just a job. A lukewarm church. A stagnant marriage. Disconnected kids. A life less than well-lived.

Is that what you were shooting for back in your early 20s? Or were you hoping for a John 10:10 kind of life? Abundant. Extreme. Full.

Paul wrote, "Let the peace of Christ rule in your

hearts, since as members of one body you were called to peace. And be thankful" (Colossians 3:15). With that in mind, let's quiet our heart while resting in an attitude of thanksgiving and revise the long paragraph above.

Here goes.

In the midst of our frantic, overloaded lives, let's remember how good we have it. And when we remember how good we have it, then we remember to thank the Supplier. And when we remember to thank the Supplier, we realize that it's not all about us. And when we realize that it's not all about us, we seek his—God's—will and guidance. And when we seek his will and guidance, we end up living for his glory. And when we live to bring glory to God, he floods our heart with joy and purpose. Contentment is the result. A job that brings new opportunities to serve him every day. A vibrant church. A fulfilling marriage. Appreciative kids. A life well-lived.

What about you?

What aspect of your life might you want to rewrite?

TAKEN BY SURPRISE

"My dear brothers and sisters, take note of this: Everyone should be quick to listen, slow to speak and slow to become angry."

JAMES 1:19

Your typically high-achieving daughter drops out of college because she's taken on too many classes in a major that really doesn't match her gifts. Your middle-schooler fakes illness because he hasn't even started his insect collection and it's due that day. Your 18-year-old son gets in a costly car accident after his insurance was canceled due to nonpayment.

And you are totally taken by surprise.

Your reaction to your now-desperate child is "Why didn't you come to me earlier? Why am I just hearing about this now? If you'd come to me I would have helped!"

Their next response is even more surprising. They say, "I did come to you, but you weren't listening." Digging through foggy memories, you do remember something about unsettled college plans, helping to catch bugs, and an overdue car insurance bill. But you were distracted or busy. Or worse, you were flippant or dismissive. Or even worse, you were gruff or angry.

Dad, you want your kids to come to you in good

times and bad. When they have news to share or conflicts to resolve, you want to be the kind of father who turns off the TV, closes the document, puts down the paper, pulls out the ear buds, lays down the tool—and turns to your son or daughter and says, "I always have time for you."

What about you?

We love to rescue our kids. We love being the hero. We love being needed. So: Be quick to listen. Slow to speak. Slow to become angry.

HEART TO HEART

"The Lord is near to the brokenhearted."

Psalm 34:18 nasb

I totally understand that Psalm 34 was not written specifically about teenage angst. But on any given day, "brokenhearted" is an accurate description of your teen. There is no doubt that the Lord is near to them. God loves your teenager. He has a plan for your teenager. He knows how much you care about your teenager. When you pray for your teenager, he hears that prayer. I believe God rejoices every time a parent prays for a child.

There are all kinds of reasons for a teenager to have a broken heart. They get dumped. They get cut from the sport they've been playing since they were six. They don't make the show choir, cast list, concert band, or debate team. Acne. Body image. Loneliness. Stress about the future. Not being invited to a social event. Their parents are separated. Their dog dies. Their friend moves away. Their favorite TV show is canceled. Their favorite T-shirt gets a bleach spot. A stranger is sitting at their favorite table at Starbucks. Some of these sorrows may seem trivial to you, but they are not to your teen.

What can a dad do? Come alongside. Don't dismiss their angst. It's very real. Actually, you do want them to come to you with their tears, frustration, anger, embarrassment, and concerns about the future. But, Dad, don't think you're required to heal their broken heart.

A wise strategy might be to remind them what Paul said to Timothy, the young pastor he had taken under his wing. "Let no one look down on your youthfulness, but rather in speech, conduct, love, faith and purity, show yourself an example of those who believe" (1 Timothy 4:12 NASB).

What about you?

Don't buy into the bad press about teenagers. That season of life can include wonderfully satisfying conversations as you start to connect with your children on an adult level. Hey, your teeneager may even begin to show some appreciation for the sacrifices you've made over the years.

PRIDE OF THE FOX

"It's a shallow life that doesn't
give a person a few scars."

Garrison Keillor

We have a 20-inch cement fox sitting in the wood chips about a foot from our front porch.

I bought it after moving into our third house and realizing this might very well be the home in which we finish raising our kids and eventually retire. It's a nice family-oriented neighborhood in St. Charles, Illinois (a.k.a. "the Pride of the Fox"—"Fox" being the Fox River), the town where Rita and I met and fell in love. I gave the cement statue to her as a Mother's Day present, not imagining she would one day be elected to the city council. Fifteen years later, it sits as a tribute to the city, our family, and God's grace.

You see, the fox has a chip in his nose. Just a few days after he was put in his place of honor, my then-three-year-old daughter, Rae Anne, attempted to use it as a stepping-stone from which to jump from the porch to the sidewalk. The fox tipped, Rae Anne tumbled, and I was more concerned about the condition of the cement statue than my own daughter. Rae Anne was fine. The fox lost a half-inch off his snout.

I wasn't happy. Luckily, my paternal instinct kept

me from blasting my innocent daughter. Really, she was just being a three-year-old. Jumping and climbing on statues is one of the things three-year-olds do best. Still, for months—maybe years—I let the chip on that fox's nose grind my gut.

The story ends this way. I got used to it. The fox's shortened nose became an endearing feature—a badge of honor earned in the battle of raising five kids.

To this day, I still notice the chipped snout just about every time I walk by. But instead of muttering, I think of and pray for Rae Anne, now enrolled at the U.S. Military Academy at West Point. Where my feisty little girl also walks by statues every day. And never thinks about jumping off them.

What about you?

In the midst of raising your family, don't let little things become too big. Or big things become too little. Life with kids leaves battle scars. Trust that time will make them beautiful.

PUTTING AWAY CHILDHOOD

"When I was a child, I spoke and thought and reasoned as a child. But when I grew up, I put away childish things. Now we see things imperfectly as in a cloudy mirror, but then we will see everything with perfect clarity. All that I know now is partial and incomplete, but then I will know everything completely, just as God now knows me completely."

1 Corinthians 13:11-12 nlt

The Bible has all kinds of rules that you can use to bash your teenager over the head. Do this. Don't do that. It's all true and it's all written for their instruction. But those rules can feel like a burden.

Wouldn't it be nice to pull out the Bible and show them a verse that makes them feel like they're headed in the right direction? Don't we all like to hear some positive reinforcement every once in a while?

Well, next time your son or daughter does something that reveals new maturity, turn to 1 Corinthians 13:11-12 and share it. It could be when they see something around the house that needs to get done and they do it themselves: mowing the lawn, cleaning the kitchen, picking up dog poop, changing a lightbulb, sorting recyclables, and so on. It could be when they voluntarily take on a new challenge outside their comfort zone: organizing a food drive, volunteering in the church nursery, tithing 10 percent of their babysitting money, taking a position of leadership in their youth group, or going out of their way to visit a grandparent, great-grandparent, or other older person.

When your child surprises you with grown-up behavior, don't be so surprised! But do take them quietly aside and say, "Hey, I noticed. And I'm glad to be your dad." Remind them there's no hurry to leave childhood behind, but it's a joy to see them growing in maturity and grace.

Remind them also that even adults don't have all the answers. But we will when we see God face-to-face.

What about you?

It's a great day when you can have an adult conversation with your child. Start early, stay connected, and you'll recognize the instant that happens.

SHARPENING RELATIONSHIPS

"As iron sharpens iron, so one person sharpens another."

PROVERBS 27:17

Last spring, I had the privilege of speaking to a small lecture hall of dads at the Iron Sharpens Iron conference in Springfield, Illinois. The room was jammed. Every seat was taken, and at least 20 more dads were either standing or sitting on the floor. I had brought a case and a half of books and sold them out.

This national ministry to men is going strong, and I recommend that every guy reading this book seek out an Iron Sharpens Iron conference in their area. And bring a friend. I shared some things, learned some things, and made some new friends. It was a great day.

But the best part of the day was that my son Isaac drove down from Peoria to spend the day with his old dad. We hung out at my booth and sold some books. During my presentation he was an effective and interactive visual aid to my fathering tales, which were sometimes about him. Afterward, we swapped stories over a well-deserved steak dinner: bone-in rib eyes.

It was a real-life example of one of my favorite

fathering principles. Enter your kids' world. And invite them to enter yours. A generation apart, fathers and their offspring live in different arenas with different cultural expectations, technologies, and challenges. Coming together with a common purpose for a day or an hour at a time helps you see the world through their eyes. And vice versa.

Over the last two decades—from being a volunteer reader in his kindergarten class to being an overnight guest at his fraternity house—I've taken advantage of dozens of opportunities to enter Isaac's world. Which may have been one of the reasons he felt comfortable and welcome to enter mine.

What about you?

Are you welcome in your child's world? Are they welcome in yours? See what you can do—early and often—to keep that invitation open both ways.

TICK. TICK. TICK. TICK.

"Love is spelled to a kid T-I-M-E."

Josh McDowell

The debate over quality time vs. quantity time is no longer debated. The expert consensus is that you really cannot expect to have any quality time with your children unless you have sufficient quantity time. The idea that we can work 70-hour weeks, ignore our kids month after month, and then make up for it with a trip to Disney World or a long weekend skiing at Aspen is a myth. Your kids may have fun in Orlando or Colorado, but it won't be with you. It will be with a stranger who happens to know their name and pay the bills.

Is that harsh? A little. For most dads, there will probably be a season of life when your job takes you away from your family for an uncomfortable number of minutes, hours, days, or weeks. It doesn't have to spell disaster. My advice is to minimize that time away, prepare to make any difficult career decisions that need to be made, and have long, heartfelt talks with your bride about what's best for the family.

What about you?

Although you can never reclaim time lost, you can

make the most of the time you do have. Rather than choose ambitious, frantic vacations, take trips that allow plenty of time to discover the countryside and your family.

DOORS OPENED EARLY

"He who began a good work in you will carry it on to completion until the day of Christ Jesus."

PHILIPPIANS 1:6

Way back in 1968, my sixth-grade class staged a production of *A Charlie Brown Christmas* for the entire school body. Most of the boys wanted to be Pig-Pen, and the girls were divided between Lucy, Sally, Violet, and Peppermint Patty.

As for me, I set my sights on the role of Linus and did something I had never done before. I memorized a portion of the Bible. Seven verses! Luke 2:8-14. It never dawned on me I was committing Scripture to memory. I thought I was simply memorizing a long speech from a script.

This 11-year-old totally nailed his audition. I started with the words, "Lights, please," continued with, "And there were in the same district, shepherds abiding in the field keeping watch over their flock by night..." and finished with the memorable line, "And that's what Christmas is all about, Charlie Brown."* It probably

* Adapted from Donald Fraser and Derrick Bang, *Security Blankets: How* Peanuts *Touched Our Lives* (Kansas City, MO: Andrews McMeel Publishing, LLC, 2009), as accessed at www.amazon.com/Security-Blankets-Peanuts-Touched-Lives/dp/0740771051#reader_0740771051.

also helped that I was one of the shorter boys in the class and already had a Linus-style haircut.

That humble production may have been a turning point in my life. I was just playing a role, but as Linus I was actually sharing the greatest news in the history of the world. Something like that can have an impact on a pre-teen.

Since then, my appreciation for the Bible and committing portions of it to memory has greatly expanded. And I have also been on stage a few times since sixth grade. As a producer for Christian radio and author of several Christian books, I can even trace my chosen career back to that performance.

All that to say, Dad, never underestimate how a door can open in middle school that changes your child's life forever.

What about you?

What childhood events pointed you toward your career, hobby, or some other rewarding aspect of your adult life? What if you had known then what you know now? Maybe share the entire story with your own kids.

CONFLICT RESOLUTION

"It is in pardoning that we are pardoned."

Francis of Assisi

You'll recognize this verse from Mark, chapter 11.

"When you stand praying, if you hold anything against anyone, forgive them, so that your Father in heaven may forgive you your sins" (Mark 11:25).

Don't know about you, but I always figured this verse was talking about some quarrel I might have had with someone I barely know. Maybe a business competitor who stole a client, the neighbor whose dog dug up my daffodils, or some creep that dinged my fender in a parking lot.

On second thought, the individuals who are most likely to need your forgiveness are the people with whom you spend the most time and who know exactly how to push your buttons: your family.

Forgiving strangers is easy. You can do it without even being in the same room or speaking a single syllable. Forgiving members of your own family is a little tougher. Your son, who reacted sarcastically to your question. Your daughter, who ignored a direct request. Your wife, who overreacted to a minor offense and won't let it go.

According to Mark 11:25, you can't get right with

God until you get right with them. Dad, as leader of the family, you need to take the first step. Get the facts. Clear up any confusion. Suggest that it's time to make things right.

Look at it this way. If you're holding something against them, there's a good chance they're holding something against you. When you take the initiative to make things right, you are very likely helping both of you get right with God.

What about you?

Leadership is not always charging ahead with drawn sword and bold war cry. In a family, leadership often requires an empathetic viewpoint—considering all sides of a disagreement and letting go of the petty issues that mean zero in the long run.

A SALUTE TO ALL ATHLETES

"You created my inmost being; you knit me together in my mother's womb."

PSALM 139:13

I recommend you get involved in Special Olympics. Volunteer. Donate. Or just show up and cheer in the stands.

My son Max and his new bride, Megan, both teach in the special education department at St. Charles East High School and care deeply for the kids in their charge. We've watched Megan coach Illinois Special Olympics (ISO) athletes, who represent the school very well. Their dedication and enthusiasm could serve as a lesson for all student athletes.

For the end-of-year ISO banquet, Megan assembled a moving video for the team, which filled the room with inspiring images, well-chosen music, cheers, and applause. In the middle of the presentation, I put my head down, sniffed back some tears, and prayed. As I have done before, I asked God for forgiveness.

You see, I have five kids who are healthy. They all attended the same high school represented by this courageous ISO team. And more times than I care to count over the last decade and a half, I have been a jerk in the stands during Alec's, Randy's, Max's, Isaac's, and Rae Anne's athletic competitions. Grousing about umpires and refs. Muttering too loudly about coaching decisions. And forgetting all the rules I taught my own kids about sportsmanship.

Gentlemen, if that also describes you, I have a three-word recommendation: Just stop it. You are more than fortunate to have a child who can and does compete. The last thing you want to do is cast a shadow over their efforts and accomplishments. Take it from someone who still has regrets in that area.

Do you know the motto of the Special Olympics? It's pretty good. And applies to every athlete at every level of competition. And it applies to dads as well:

> *"Let me win. But if I cannot win, let me be brave in the attempt."*

What about you?

What are you doing to teach your children the value of sportsmanship? What are you doing to teach your children the value of life?

THE VALUE OF PAUSING

"A voice from heaven said, 'This is my Son, whom I love; with him I am well pleased.'"

MATTHEW 3:17

Rita and I were both raised in a traditional church environment. Following the practice of our upbringing, our five children were all baptized as infants. The ceremonies were meaningful and joyous.

Over the years, we never missed a Sunday, developed a warm and gracious relationship with the pastoral staff, invested time and resources, and built many lifelong friendships through our church family. Still, we came to the conclusion that our young family needed more Bible teaching and less ritual. We needed to count more on convictions and less on tradition.

Our parents were not delighted to see us leave their denomination, and we understood where they were coming from. But once we had moved to the big nondenominational church on the edge of town, we knew it was the right decision. We soaked up the in-depth Bible teaching and dug into small-group studies. We also witnessed adult baptisms for the first time.

After getting plugged into youth group, our oldest son, Alec, came to the conviction that he wanted to get dunked in order to demonstrate publicly that he had put his faith and trust in Jesus. Rita and I were encouraging to him, but we didn't know how that would sit with our more traditional parents.

Here's the point of this little story. (And I hope the lesson rings true for all dads.) We told my dad that his grandson—who had been sprinkled 15 years earlier—was going to get full-immersion baptized. My father paused thoughtfully for several moments and finally said, "Well, if it was good enough for Jesus, it's good enough for my grandson."

I will be eternally grateful to my dad for that thoughtful, compassionate, and generous response.

What about you?

When one of your kids comes to you with a new way of thinking, will you instantly go off the deep end? Or will you pause long enough to get the facts and consider the big picture?

THY WILL BE DONE

"Since God offers to manage our affairs for us, let us once and for all hand them over to His infinite wisdom, in order to occupy ourselves only with Himself and what belongs to Him."

JEAN-PIERRE DE CAUSSADE

It's a good sign when your son or daughter asks, "How can I know what God wants me to do with my life?" But how do you answer?

Try this: Explain that God's will can be divided into two categories. God's universal will for all people. And God's specific will for each of us as individuals.

God's universal will is given to us in the Bible. Things like "flee immorality," "do not be yoked with unbelievers," "let God's Word dwell in you," "honor your father and mother," and scores of other directives that are explicit and clear, and take a lifetime to pursue.

God's specific will for your child is a little tougher to discern. It's all about those questions unique to your child's life: Who to date? Should I join the military? Which college major? Should I go to Florida on spring break?

Well here's an answer that seems simple, but it's biblically sound. Tell your child to sincerely and diligently pursue God's *universal* will and that should lead to a clear understanding of God's *specific* will. As a matter of fact, Psalm 37:4 promises, "Delight yourself in the LORD; and He will give you the desires of your heart" (NASB).

In other words, pursue God with all your heart and then do *whatever your heart tells you to do*.

Warning, Dad: Don't tell this to any child who is not pursuing God's universal will. They'll take it as a free pass to do anything *they* want.

What about you?

We want to be able to give our kids exact answers to their questions. Sometimes the answer is, "Do what you already know is pleasing to God."

MAIL MEN

"Letters are expectation packaged in an envelope."

Shana Alexander

Text your kids. E-mail. Message them on Facebook. *But not too often.* You don't want to be a stalker or creeper. That can happen before you know it with digital media. It's almost too easy to communicate, even with fat dad thumbs and a complete ignorance of most of the abbreviations and emoticons. You want to enter their world, not invade it. In general, most of your texts should actually be responding to theirs. A good rule when communicating with your kids in the electronic age: Leave them wanting more.

One form of communication you probably cannot overdo is the written word—on actual paper—including notes, clippings, and cards in envelopes stamped and sealed with a kiss. Letters are rare and beautiful things.

Want proof? Read the first few verses of Romans, 1 and 2 Corinthians, Galatians, Ephesians, Philippians, Colossians, 1 and 2 Thessalonians, and so on. Paul wrote those letters to challenge, correct, and instruct faith communities, but he always started with some wonderfully encouraging prose. See if you can count how many times Paul writes, "I thank God every time I think about you." Or something like that. You can be sure those letters were appreciated and cherished by those new groups of believers.

Dad, if you have kids out of the house for a week, a semester, or until they run out of money, think about dropping them a note. Unlike Mom, you don't need fancy stationery. But you do need their address and a first-class stamp. Don't forget to begin each letter—like Paul—"I thank God every time I think about you."

By the way, if you're in a situation where you're forced to live away from your children, then you already know the importance of letters and packages. Keep it going, Dad. You may not always get a response, but your mail is always appreciated.

We dads are probably not going to save the U.S. Postal Service. But we can save our kids from feeling disconnected from the family.

What about you?

Writing letters dramatically increases the chance that you will receive letters. And if you haven't received any letters recently, go back and read those epistles from Paul. They weren't just written to churches and individuals of the first century. They were also written to you.

JUST SAY IT

"A word fitly spoken is like apples of gold in settings of silver."

Proverbs 25:11 NKJV

I could say, "I don't mean to put words in your mouth." But actually that's exactly what I'm trying to do. I know you already say, "Have a great day," to your kids as they head out the door. You may even say "Sweet dreams" or "Sleep tight" at the end of the day. But maybe it's time to mix it up a bit and add a few more expressions to your spoken-word repertoire. In the next few days, try a few of these fathering phrases out on your kids.

"You make me smile."

"I am so proud of you."

"Where did you learn to do that? That's fantastic."

"I look around and can't believe how lucky I am to be part of this family."

"You are a gift from God."

"You're amazing."

"You did that! That's epic."

"Well played."

"You probably don't even realize how much your little brother looks up to you."

"Hey, what's the biggest thing on your mind right now?"

"Hey, sweetheart, come over here and tell me about your day."

"Hey, champ, come over here and tell me about your day."

"You are just about the best thing that ever happened to me!"

"That's a great idea. I wish I had thought of it."

"I was thinking about you all day today."

"How did that geography quiz go?"

"You know what? I love you."

Words from a father may be one of the most powerful forces in the life of a child. I encourage you, Dad, to choose now to use that power only for good. Be well aware that words spoken to your child can also be used to destroy.

What about you?

What words and phrases from your own father are echoing in your head? Hopefully they're all good, but even the best dads leave some verbal scars. If necessary, talk it out with a trusted friend and let those words go. Never to be heard again.*

---

* This selection adapted from Jay Payleitner, *365 Ways to Say "I Love You" to Your Kids* (Eugene, OR: Harvest House Publishers, 2011).

LESS FUSS, LESS MUSS

"As a child my family's menu consisted of two choices: take it, or leave it."

Buddy Hackett

Our kids were not fussy eaters. But one of them really, really didn't like asparagus. Actually, none of the kids liked asparagus.

But during one particular dinner, one particular kid let it be known that there was no way he was going to eat his asparagus. In my fatherly wisdom, I let it be known that he was not going to leave the dinner table without eating that asparagus—all four spears. It was a classic dinner-table standoff. I was serious and committed. So was he.

Truth be told, I like asparagus when it's steamed, buttered, and still hot. But—as you'll probably agree—cold and mushy asparagus is something on which to gag. And that's exactly what the young diner did. He sat there for several minutes, gave me the evil eye for several more, and finally shoved two or three cold, soggy asparagus spears into his mouth. Gagging, choking, and spitting some of the green goo back onto his plate.

That's all I remember. I don't recall how the incident ended. I don't remember if there was a prolonged standoff at the dining room table or any additional punishment. I do remember suggesting to Rita that we quietly avoid serving asparagus for a while. We didn't tell that to the kids, but it just seemed like a battle we didn't want to fight again for a few months. And that was that.

The lasting impact of the event is really the most amusing part of the story. As adults, all our children enjoy fresh asparagus, even ordering it in restaurants. When the plates are presented, one of the kids always says in mock seriousness, "No one leaves this table until you finish your asparagus."

What about you?

Other than their birthday, I hope you're not letting your kids dictate your dinner menu. On the other hand, I also hope you're not waging a spite-filled relationship-damaging war with your kids on trivial matters such as asparagus, ripped jeans, toothpaste on the sink, elbows on the table, loading the dishwasher the wrong way, or not stacking the newspapers in a neat pile. Dad, we need to pick our battles more carefully than that.

LOVE THE LITTLE ONES

"See that you do not despise one of these little ones. For I tell you that their angels in heaven always see the face of my Father in heaven."

Matthew 18:10

My bride likes to hold babies. Rita is also vocal about her pro-life stand. And she doesn't just talk about stuff she cares about, she puts her words into action.

All of which explains why we became state-approved foster parents. With my blessing and partnership, we went through the classes, did the background check and fingerprints, and put our name on the list of accredited foster homes, signifying that we would take newborns and also that we were not intending to adopt.

We were told it might be months before our first placement. It was hours. Because of the confidentiality laws, I can't tell you much except that we had that little guy for almost exactly a year. Just after his first birthday, we turned him over to a wonderful forever family with whom we still keep in touch. It was very hard. But it was awesome. I give Rita credit—and so do his mom and dad—for teaching that little baby boy how to love. And how to be loved. She held him constantly, and that's a great way to go through the first year of life.

We made two discoveries that year. First, parents

can love an adopted child just as much as they love the kids who share their genetic makeup. And second, there is no such thing as an unwanted child.

Since that initial fostering experience, we've been privileged to welcome nine other newborns into our home for various lengths of time. Several were addicted to cocaine because their birth mothers had been crack users. As a family, we all had the disturbing experience of holding those babies while they shivered through cocaine withdrawal. By the way, comforting a helpless infant through coke-induced tremors is a pretty strong antidrug message for teenagers.

All that to say, if your bride has a true calling, don't be surprised if it impacts your entire family.

What about you?

Foster dads. Adoptive dads. Stepdads. Single dads. You're all dads. And every bit of advice holds true across the board. Especially this: One of your most important jobs is to teach each of your children how to love and how to be loved.

POSSESSIONS THAT POSSESS

"The rich man is not one who is in possession of much, but one who gives much."

John Chrysostom

There's satisfaction in making an honest living and providing for your loved ones. A day of good honest sweat leads to a good night's sleep. Crooks and con men don't have sweet dreams.

Still, at the end of the day what you do for a living cannot be the sum total of what you are in life. You can love your job (and I hope you do). But don't love the money that comes with it. Otherwise, it controls you. First Timothy 6:10 famously asserts, "The love of money is a root of all kinds of evil."

Escalating greed seems to be a mark of our society, as well as most societies in history. In almost every case, in the end, greed consumes and destroys. The more we have, the more we have to worry about. The bigger the house, the more critical the locks and alarms. Finely tuned Maseratis and Porsches require constant fine tuning. (At least that's what I've heard.) More stuff, more stress.

How can a working man keep possessions from

possessing him? First, have less stuff. Second, eliminate or gain control over debt. But the best way to keep money from consuming you is to give some of it away. Hey, in the grand scheme of things it's not really yours anyway.

Once you've mastered the art of giving, take another more dramatic step. Try giving *in secret*—generously, magnanimously, without taking credit or telling anyone. Keeping it just between you and God.

What about you?

I am no financial guru. But there are excellent Christian financial experts and counselors available. Your pastor can point you in the right direction.

HIDDEN IN THEIR HEART—AND YOURS

"How can a young person stay on the path of purity? By living according to your word. I seek you with all my heart; do not let me stray from your commands. I have hidden your word in my heart that I might not sin against you."

PSALM 119:9-11

One of the coolest things that can ever happen to you is to struggle with an issue and then have a Bible verse pop into your head that exactly answers that question. It's like, "Thank You, God—now I know what to do."

God works that way sometimes. But really, when that happens, you can take some of the credit. Somewhere along the way you put yourself in a position to be exposed to that portion of Scripture. It may have been sitting in a pew or in Sunday school, reading a bumper sticker or needlepoint, doing personal Bible study, or listening to your mom or dad when you were a kid.

Which brings us to a worthy goal for any dad. Do memory verses with your kids—at any age. Here are a few to start with.

- Kids love this one:

  I can do all this through him who gives me strength (Philippians 4:13).

- Parents love this one:

  Children, obey your parents in everything, for this pleases the Lord (Colossians 3:20).

- This verse reminds kids that how they act relates to the life of Jesus:

  Be kind and compassionate to one another, forgiving each other, just as in Christ God forgave you (Ephesians 4:32).

- These passages are core to the idea of sin, grace, and salvation:

  All have sinned and fall short of the glory of God (Romans 3:23).

  God demonstrates his own love for us in this: While we were still sinners, Christ died for us (Romans 5:8).

  Jesus answered, "I am the way and the truth and the life. No one comes to the Father except through me" (John 14:6).

  God so loved the world that he gave his one and only Son, that whoever believes in him shall not perish but have eternal life (John 3:16).

- Here's another one that seems to resonate with kids:

  Love the Lord *your God with all your heart and with all your soul and with all your strength (Deuteronomy 6:5).*

Help your children hide God's Word in their hearts and you just might be equipping them with tools that will rescue them when you're not around.

What about you?

Most of the verses I know word for word are a direct result of practicing Awana verses with my kids. And later being an Awana leader.* It's good stuff and good times.

---

* Awana is an international evangelical nonprofit organization whose mission is to help "churches and parents worldwide raise children and youth to know, love and serve Christ." Awana licenses its curricula to any church willing to pay for and use its materials in accord with its principles. The Awana name is derived from the first letters of "Approved workmen are not ashamed," adapted from 2 Timothy 2:15. See more at awana.org.

THE MEASURE OF A MAN

"Jesus grew in wisdom and stature,
and in favor with God and man."

Luke 2:52

My Aunt Carolyn and Uncle Donny passed away years ago. Their basement rec room was where my family spent Christmas Eve during my growing-up years. Beyond the gifts and the fellowship, three images come instantly to mind when I think about that annual gathering.

One, the corner of the room filled with giant trophies earned by the Racine Scouts drum-and-bugle corps. Two, the beautifully garish shiny aluminum Christmas tree illuminated by a rotating translucent color wheel. Three, the stud wall behind the basement door, on which all the cousins marked our heights every year.

It really is an eye-opening moment when a child realizes he has literally grown in the last year. I remember stretching myself up so that the pencil mark would be as high as possible. The archive of lines accompanied by names and dates was proof I had grown physically from Christmas Eve to Christmas Eve.

Aunt Carolyn would always make a fuss about how much we had grown. I remember also how the pencil marks on the stud wall annually confirmed that I was not catching up with my brother Mark and probably never would.

But grow in wisdom and stature I did. Not as tall as I would have liked. Not as wise either. Any physical growth stopped decades ago. As for wisdom, I'm going to let you readers decide for yourself.

Dad, as the years go by make sure your kids receive plenty of nourishment and physical exercise to grow in stature. That's something you can actually measure. With marks on a stud wall once a year.

But make sure they also grow in wisdom. That's not as easy to quantify, so you'll have to stay close and see how they're progressing each and every day.

What about you?

Find a wall behind a door and line your kids up and mark their height. Let them know you look forward to watching them grow. In wisdom, stature, and favor with God and man.

GOT BIG GOALS?

"It is not enough to take steps which may some day lead to a goal; each step must be itself a goal and a step likewise."

JOHANN WOLFGANG VON GOETHE

What jazzes you? What floats your boat? Is there something in your life that gets you out of bed in the morning with purpose and determination? Do you have a personal mission statement that gives you a daily green light reminding you to go after it?

More important than the green light, does that mission statement have a red-light clause? Do you know when enough is enough? If you don't know when you've reached your goal, when do you stop running? When is enough, enough?

The idea of goal-setting is especially important for dads. But be careful. Don't set your goals using a floating scale. Too many men spend their life trying to keep up with their neighbors. But as soon as they catch up, they change neighborhoods. They move to a bigger house surrounded by even bigger houses and greener lawns. Consider this passage from Philippians.

> *I have learned to be content whatever the circumstances. I know what it is to be in need, and I*

know what it is to have plenty. I have learned the secret of being content in any and every situation, whether well fed or hungry, whether living in plenty or in want (Philippians 4:11-12).

Learning contentment is actually a wise survival skill for today's competitive world. Some other guy will always have a bigger house, higher-achieving kids, or a better-looking wife.

I hope you've positioned a long bright avenue of green lights in your life. Signals that say "go" are invaluable when it comes to reaching worthy life goals. But I also hope you position some yellow and red lights along the way to remind you to enjoy the scenery and smell the flowers.

Perhaps the ultimate goal is to be able to walk in your door at the end of the day and be able to say, "It's good to be home. This home. With this family."

What about you?

Making a list of goals is a good thing. Even aggressive goals that require hard work and superior intelligence. But on your list of goals make sure to include things like "happy wife," "happy kids," and "humility."

BIG-PICTURE THINKING

"I've read the last page of the Bible. It's going to turn out all right."

Billy Graham

We could take Reverend Graham literally here and turn to the last chapter of Revelation. There, Jesus confirms that he is the Alpha and Omega, the beginning and the end. In the last two verses he testifies, "Yes, I am coming soon." Then the apostle John ends the Bible with the words "Amen. Come, Lord Jesus. The grace of the Lord Jesus be with God's people. Amen."

As usual, Billy is accurate. When Jesus returns everything is going to be all right.

As a dad, though, I want to do more than just point my kids to the last page of the Bible. There's work to be done while we wait for the second coming. I want my kids to engage in living for eternity—a concept that's going to help them in every decision they ever make.

Indeed, we can take comfort in knowing that everything is going to turn out just as God planned. But we can also take courage in that truth. As we pursue his will in our life, we can move forward with confidence, knowing he will light our path, he will feed us in the desert, he will rescue us from demons if we simply call on his name. We can live fully because we are ready to die confidently.

When we get to the last page of the Bible, we need to be able to close the genuine imitation leather binding, embrace the big picture of the book that extends beyond mere words on a page, and say, "Yes, this is worth living and worth dying for."

What about you?

Are your kids living for today? Or have you taught them to look beyond today and beyond themselves? Big-picture thinking looks forward to the time when God makes all things new. The old ways (our ways) will be revealed to be an illusion. Heaven is the only reality that matters.

FOREVER A DAD

"The Lord is good and his love endures forever; his faithfulness continues through all generations."

Psalm 100:5

When is a dad no longer a dad? The answer is never. If you've loved on a newborn, taught a five-year-old to ride a bike, given the birds-and-bees talk, handed over car keys to a new driver, or stood in the bedroom doorway of your grown child after they've moved out on their own, you are forever a dad.

And the world needs dads. Good ones like you. Dads establish a strong foundation of faith, sort out messes, protect children from nasty influences, and mold mushy young minds into clear-thinking adult ones.

When your kids are no longer living under your roof, their needs have changed, but you are still a valuable part of their life. You've bought homes and cars. They haven't. You've replaced water heaters, caulked windows, and bought life insurance. They haven't. You have a good idea about what home repairs to do yourself and when to call in a professional. You have tools they don't and patience they need. So just when you think your dad skills are obsolete, you're really entering an entirely new phase of your father–child relationship.

If that's not enough fathering responsibility, don't

forget that there's an entire generation of fatherless kids out there dreaming, wishing, and praying for a dad like you. Every kid needs a father figure with a moral compass and a faith worth passing on.

An even more powerful way to help hurting kids might be to come alongside men who are already fathers but feel overwhelmed by the task. By mentoring a young dad or two, you can multiply your experience over and over again.

Finally, just when you start thinking your daddying days are over, your son or daughter presents you with the next generation. And you get a whole new name: Gramps.

What about you?

There will come a time when you can no longer be there. To prepare your children and grandchildren, make sure they know this great truth: They have always been and always will be under the love and care of their heavenly Father.

About the Author

Jay Payleitner is a dad. But he pays his mortgage and feeds his family working as a freelance writer, ad man, speaker, creativity trainer, and radio producer with credits including *Josh McDowell Radio*, *WordPower*, *Jesus Freaks Radio,* and *Today's Father with Carey Casey*. Jay served as the Executive Director for the Illinois Fatherhood Initiative and is a featured writer/blogger for the National Center for Fathering. He is the author of the bestselling *52 Things Kids Need from a Dad, 365 Ways to Say "I Love You" to Your Kids, The One-Year Life Verse Devotional, 40 Days to Your Best Life for Men*, and the acclaimed modern parable *Once Upon a Tandem*. Jay and his high-school sweetheart, Rita, have four sons, one daughter, and three daughters-in-law and live in St. Charles, Illinois. You can read his weekly dadblog or contact him at jaypayleitner.com.

The National Center for Fathering

We believe *every* child needs a dad they can count on. At the National Center for Fathering, we inspire and equip men to be the involved fathers, stepfathers, grandfathers, and father figures their children need.

The National Center was founded by Dr. Ken Canfield in 1990 as a nonprofit scientific and education organization. Today, under the leadership of CEO Carey Casey, we continue to provide practical, research-based training and resources that reach more than one million dads annually.

We focus our work in four areas, all of which are described in detail at fathers.com:

Research. The Personal Fathering Profile, developed by a team of researchers led by Ken Canfield, and other ongoing research projects provide fresh insights for fathers and serve as benchmarks for evaluating the effectiveness of our programs and resources.

Training. Through Championship Fathering Experiences, Father-Daughter Summits, online training, small-group curricula, and train-the-trainer programs, we have equipped over 80,000 fathers and more than 1000 trainers to impact their own families and local communities.

Programs. The National Center provides leading edge, turnkey fathering programs, including WATCH D.O.G.S.

(Dads Of Great Students), which involves dads in their children's education and is currently in more than 1300 schools in 36 states. Other programs include Fathering Court, which helps dads with significant child-support arrearages, and our annual Father of the Year Essay Contest.

Resources. Our website provides a wealth of resources for dads in nearly every fathering situation, many of them available free of charge. Dads who make a commitment to Championship Fathering receive a free weekly e-newsletter full of timely and practical tips on fathering. *Today's Father*, Carey Casey's daily radio program, airs on 600-plus stations. Listen to programs online or download podcasts at fathers.com/radio.

Make your commitment to Championship Fathering

Championship Fathering is an effort to change the culture for today's children and the children of coming generations. We're seeking to reach, teach, and unleash 6.5 million dads, creating a national movement of men who will commit to LOVE their children, COACH their children, MODEL for their children, ENCOURAGE other children, and ENLIST other dads to join the team. To make the Championship Fathering commitment, visit fathers.com/cf.

Also by Jay Payleitner

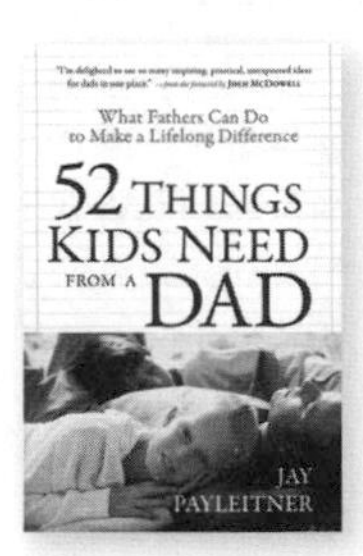

52 Things Kids Need from a Dad
What Fathers Can Do to Make a Lifelong Difference

Good news—you are already the perfect dad for your kids! Still, you know you can grow. In the pages of this bestseller, Jay Payleitner, veteran radio producer and dad of five, offers a bounty of inspiring and unexpected insights:

- *straightforward rules*: "carry photos of your kids," "Dad tucks in," and "kiss your wife in the kitchen"
- *candid advice that may be tough to hear*: "get right with your own dad," "throw out your porn," and "surrender control of the TV remote"
- *weird topics that at first seem absurd*: "buy Peeps," "spin a bucket over your head" and "rent a dolphin"

Surely, God—our heavenly Father—designed fatherhood to be a joy, a blessing, and a blast! *A great gift or men's group resource.*

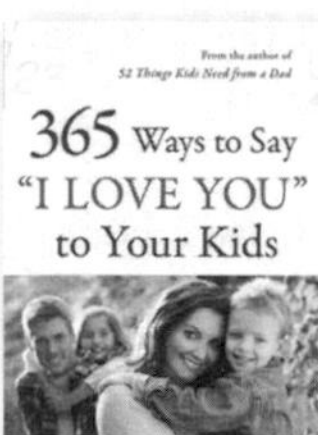

365 Ways to Say "I Love You" to Your Kids

Expressions of love can get lost in the crush of carpools, diaper changes, homework, and afterschool activities. But Jay Payleitner is here to help you turn the dizzying array of activities into great memories. Learn to say "I love you"...

> *...at bedtime...in the car...in different languages... without words...doing chores...when your kids mess up big-time...on vacation...using secret phrases...in crazy unexpected ways...in everyday life...in ways that point to God.*

Whether your kids are newborn or college-bound, these 365 simple suggestions—from silly to serious—will help you lead your precious pack to joy, laughter, and connection one "I love you" at a time.

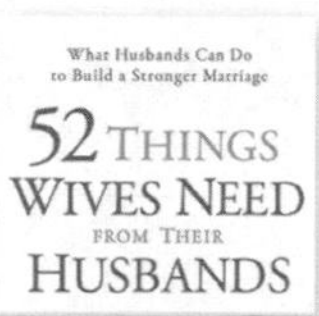

52 Things Wives Need from Their Husbands

What Husbands Can Do to Build a Stronger Marriage

Nobody knows your wife like you do. You're the guy who can make her day or break her heart. The choice is yours.

If you feel your husband technique could use a quick refresher course, look no further. Jay Payleitner, husband of Rita, veteran dad of five, and author of the bestselling *52 Things Kids Need from a Dad*, offers a bounty of man-friendly advice, such as

- "Stir her pots"
- "Surprise her with sparkly gifts"
- "Be the handyman"
- "Stay married"
- "Kiss her in the kitchen"
- "Leave your mommy"
- "Put her second"

From breakfast to bedtime. For newlyweds to empty-nesters. Here's a great and godly start to winning your wife's heart all over again!

Also from Harvest House Publishers

Daily in Christ
Neil T. Anderson

Are you fed up with trying to live the Christian life out of your own strength? Do you want to grasp a higher purpose—the reality that you are in Christ?

Neil Anderson, bestselling author of *The Bondage Breaker®*, helps you root your faith deeply in the truth of God's Word and in Christ Himself. In this one-year devotional, you'll discover day by day what it means to be a child of God—and how that identity can powerfully impact the way you live, think, and relate to those around you.

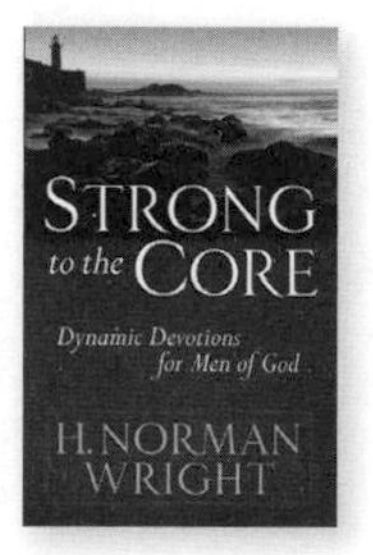

Strong to the Core
Dynamic Devotions for Men of God
H. Norman Wright

Bestselling author Norm Wright has a proven plan to help you strengthen your core—your spiritual life, your family life, and your personal life. In these short devotions, you'll find biblical truth, wisdom for bringing about growth in your relationships, and time-tested advice for working through life issues and building your friendship with God.

Norm's professional knowledge coupled with practical insights from his many years as a respected Christian counselor will encourage you to embrace God's call to live for Him, represent Him, and take a stand for Him. See how He will make a difference through you!